Great Grandpa Shorty
Great Grandma Lois

Merry XMAS
1994 -

We ♡ U!

Rod, Lyn, & Morgan

OELWEIN IA.

A BUR OAK ORIGINAL

BY MARY BENNETT

An Iowa Album

A PHOTOGRAPHIC HISTORY, 1860–1920

University of Iowa Press Iowa City

University of Iowa Press, Iowa City 52242

Copyright © 1990 by the University of Iowa

All rights reserved

Printed in the United States of America

First edition, 1990

Design by Richard Hendel

Printed on acid-free paper

Library of Congress Cataloging-in-
Publication Data

Bennett, Mary (Mary J.)
    An Iowa album: a photographic history,
1860–1920/by Mary Bennett.—1st ed.
        p.   cm. — (A Bur Oak original)
    Includes bibliographical references.
    Includes index.
    ISBN 0-87745-253-9 (alk. paper)
    1. Iowa—Description and travel—1846–
1950—Views.   2. Iowa—History—Pictorial
works.   I. Title.   II. Series.
F622.B46   1990   90-35493
977.7'02—dc20   CIP

To my grandmother

HILMA JOHNSON RYE

1891–1985

CONTENTS

ACKNOWLEDGMENTS

I could probably trace my decision to write this book to my father's love of history and my mother's talent for teaching. A more powerful motivation came from the compelling archive of historical photographs I worked with day after day. These images had the magical ability to transport me back in time and challenged me to find ways of sharing Iowa's rich photographic legacy with others. Joyce Giaquinta played a pivotal role, first by granting me the freedom to explore the potential of the long-neglected collection at the State Historical Society of Iowa and then by giving me the support and encouragement to make this book a reality.

I am grateful for the guidance I received from Elwood Parry, former professor of art history at the University of Iowa, who taught a course on the history of photography and shared many insights with me. I also owe a debt to several professors from the University of Iowa who shaped my ideas about history, in particular Malcolm Rohrbough, Sarah Hanley, Linda K. Kerber, Stow Persons, Ellis W. Hawley, Robert Dykstra, and H. Shelton Stromquist. Robert F. Sayre deserves credit for bringing the manuscript to the attention of the publisher.

Through my fifteen years of work at the State Historical Society of Iowa, a number of colleagues and associates shared ideas and were patient with me. I owe thanks to Sharlane Grant, Margaret Atherton Bonney, Bonnie Lindemann, Charlene Hixon, Irving Weber, Johnathan Lantz Buffalo, Lowell Soike, and Alan Schroder. Merle Davis, Marvin Bergman, and Jan Nash made valuable comments on the manuscript. Merle Davis deserves special commendation for constantly sharing information, especially the newspaper research for the quotations that appear in chapter 3. Other co-workers who merit recognition include Karen Laughlin, Susan Rogers, Linda Brown-Link, Becki Peterson, Christie Dailey, Mary Homeier, Matthew Carpenter, Ilene Hammond, Janet Godwin, and JeanNette Buffington Wieser.

The development of the Society's photograph collection came through the efforts of more than twenty-five student assistants and volunteers who worked to make these images accessible to researchers. Among these were Tom Doyle, James E. Scott, Sarah

Cartwright, James Hamann, Susan Daniels, Keith Eiten, Lynda Karley, James Beranek, Cynthia Coe, Amy Lilienfeld, and Jack Coyier.

Dedicated citizens like Paul Juhl, John Zeller, Bill Witt, Jo Ann Burgess, Frederick Crane, John Jacobs, Keith Kelley, and Joan Liffring-Zug work privately to preserve Iowa's photographic heritage. I am grateful for their enthusiasm and for the hours spent sharing their discoveries.

The fine photographic work in this book can be attributed to Robert A. Ryan, Sarah Dennett, and J. Ceronie of Dennett, Muessig, and Associates and to Don Roberts, Craig Kohl, Lloyd Bender, and Linda Edge-Dunlap at the University of Iowa Photographic Service.

With few exceptions, the photographs in this book came from the photograph collection of the State Historical Society of Iowa in Iowa City. Several people assisted in locating photographs for the book, including Scott Sorensen of the Sioux City Public Museum; Genie Radcliff of Alleman, Iowa; the Brott family, who loaned photographs from the E. M. Clark Collection; Constance Walther, who loaned the original nitrate negatives from the Gabelmann Collection; and George Goeldner and Thomas Jones, Jr., who graciously loaned photographs from their private collections.

This project was made possible in part by a grant from the National Endowment for the Humanities, though the views expressed do not necessarily represent those of the Endowment.

Finally, I am indebted to my companion, Robert Burchfield, who helped immeasurably.

PREFACE

Photographs can enhance our awareness of the fundamental cultural changes that occurred in Iowa in the years from 1860 to 1920. During these years, a locally oriented, traditional rural society was transformed into a more diverse and outward-looking society, tied even more closely to an emerging national culture. Change was constant—in agricultural and household technology, in farm prices and income, and in transportation, which promoted settlement and fostered the development of an industrial base. Changes in the makeup and character of the community sometimes altered Iowans' perceptions of the world. The economic and cultural patterns of life on Iowa's farms and in its small towns were modified as telephones, electricity, automobiles, movies, and radios became widely available. The complex relationship between town and country and their integration into the regional and national economy determined the context of Iowa life.

A glimpse of Iowa in this period has been captured in the images created by professional and amateur photographers. Through the eyes of those who lived during that time, we can see some of the experiences of Iowans. Sometimes a visual image can help us connect with a lost or nearly forgotten memory. This pictorial record creates an impression of the Iowa that existed when our grandparents and great-grandparents lived, but the stories our ancestors told and the events they recorded by more traditional means must be consulted before we can find meaning and insight in the images.

As an archivist, I bring primary-source materials to the attention of others so they can examine and analyze them. More sophisticated, in-depth historical studies provide the rich interpretive context for these images. Exacting descriptions of the events and forces that shaped life in rural and small-town Iowa are widely available. The work of historians like Lewis Atherton, Leland L. Sage, Dorothy Schwieder, Thomas J. Morain, and Richard Lingeman provide the perfect complement to these images. They investigate the more complex political and economic themes and shifting cultural paradigms of the era, helping to shed light on our visual heritage.

All place-names refer to Iowa unless otherwise noted. The photograph captions refer to original information on the historical photographs or negative sleeves. The captions give a description of the photograph and the source of the original image. Measurements are given if the original photograph was available or if the image came from a glass plate negative; all measurements are in inches, with the height given first. All photographs come from the collections of the State Historical Society of Iowa in Iowa City unless other institutions or individuals are cited. Reproductions of the photographs may be obtained by writing to the State Historical Society of Iowa, 402 Iowa Avenue, Iowa City, Iowa 52240.

INTRODUCTION

Through historical photographs we can better understand certain aspects of life in Iowa from 1860 to 1920, but there is much that is not revealed. The images exhibited here illustrate our common cultural heritage. Professional and amateur photographers captured a glimpse of life in Iowa's countryside and towns, and it is through their eyes that we see the world in which our ancestors lived. These illuminating documents help us explore the experiences of past generations, but the investigation is incomplete unless other sources are consulted. The recorded memories and narrative expressions taken from historical manuscripts provide a "voice" to go with the images. Together these forms of documentation create a portrait of Iowa that affirms our ideas about the past and at the same time raises new questions and draws attention to unnoticed themes.

Photography has been an integral part of our society since its invention in 1839. The ability to capture a single moment in time had previously been limited to artists, whose renderings could seldom match the accuracy, realism, and exactness of photography. The "truthful" image could document life, possessing a timeless quality that challenged and changed long-standing perceptions of the world. The scientific wonder of photography became a universal medium for recording life, creating a new visual language for understanding culture that could be used for artistic expression or for documenting and interpreting historical processes. The very fact that photography became so accessible to the masses made it a unique new form of communication, one that would affect the society emerging out of the nineteenth century in a profound and immeasurable way. Photography, drawing on older pictorial arts, paved the way for the visual expression so dominant in modern society.

But photography, though heralded for its realistic, mechanical viewpoint, contains contradictory elements as well, for the camera can create illusions. Photography is at once both objective and subjective: objective in the sense that it perfectly replicates the scene before it, but subjective because the photographer controls the image by selecting the subject matter to record. Photographers can alter a composition or frame the subject in such a way as to create an emotional human response. In expressing a personal vision of the world, the bias of the photographer and his or her relationship to the subject portrayed is of primary importance in determining the outcome of the image.

Commercial and professional photographers have deliberately chosen their range of subjects in response to their customers' desires or because someone commissioned them to take the photographs. As the extensive collection of images presented here attests, local photographers have been dedicated to recording life in the town and the surrounding community. The informal photos taken by amateur photographers sometimes catch people off guard, inadvertently documenting scenes that were not meant to be recorded. Though photographers did not record every moment, their images do help to clarify our understanding of daily routines and the surrounding environment. People intended to portray the parts of their lives that they were proud of—their aspirations and achievements as well as the momentous times in their lives. The special quality of family snapshots—even if they are off-center or slightly blurred—is that they catch people in ordinary everyday activities among family and intimate friends. Moreover, they depict many facets of the private lives, as well as the public roles, of our ancestors.

One needs to combine imagination with careful observation when "reading" a photograph. The viewer should not jump to conclusions but should consider the photographer's intent and the attributes of the equipment and techniques she or he employed. Whatever inspired the photographer, along with the means available to record the images, holds the key to understanding the life surrounding that moment in time. Each photograph must be put into context by examining other historical materials relating to the time it was taken. The photograph is but one source of documentation, though perhaps ultimately the one that reveals many more subtle characteristics of history than do written forms of documentation.

Iowa's historical past can be seen in a more textured, more meaningful way through imagery. Photographs have the power to recreate the past in visual terms and convey the human spirit that plays such an important part in historical processes. We can sense a continuity of traditions and see attitudes and customs revealed in a personal way. Images show the common bonds between our lives and the lives of past generations. Those images that survive are treasures from our cultural past and must be collected and preserved so that we can be more fully aware of the varied dimensions of our ancestors' lives.

CHAPTER I : INDIANS AND THE LAND

The pristine condition of Iowa's primeval forests, waterways, and prairie landscape was barely altered by centuries of habitation by Native Americans. But the bountiful natural environment that had sustained various tribes was tamed and profitably modified by successive generations of settlers. Both groups maintained a close association with the land not simply for its practical value but because life itself followed nature's seasonal rhythms. Early visitors were enthralled by the expansive prairie vistas of tall grasses and delicate wildflowers. Covering three-fourths of the state, prairie savannas were broken by stands of oak, hickory, and walnut along meandering rivers and streams. The woodland sanctuaries lining the valleys and skirting the hillsides sheltered animals and humans from intense heat and cold. Careful observers have seen the intrinsic beauty and dramatic power of nature revealed in a variety of ways. Isolating blizzards, floods that can come without warning, and long summers without adequate rain have been real tests of survival; but overall, the land has provided the sustenance of Iowa's economic and cultural life.

People have inhabited Iowa for thousands of years. The Native Americans who originally settled in this region were members of as many as seventeen tribes, though at the time Euro-Americans reached the area there were six primary tribes: the Dakota or Sioux in the northwest; the Iowa in the central area along the Des Moines River; the Sauk and Mesquakie (Fox), who migrated to the eastern portion from Illinois and Wisconsin; the Winnebago, who were temporarily placed in the northeast corner of the territory and later moved to Nebraska; and the Potawatami, who were moved to southwestern Iowa. Of these tribes, only the Mesquakie were able to withstand the enormous pressures of the advancing frontier with the myriad intrusions by the federal government and pioneer settlers.

The woodland Indians in the eastern part of the state based their livelihood on agriculture and seasonal hunts. Tribes lived in communities of wickiups made from woven mats of reeds gathered from riverbanks. Women gardened, harvested fruits and nuts, and tended to domestic needs, while men hunted and fished or waged limited war against enemy tribes. The more nomadic Indians on the plains of western Iowa lived in

The edge of the forest meets the prairie in Buena Vista County in the 1890s. Samuel Calvin, photographer; 5 × 8 glass plate negative, Geology Department, University of Iowa.

tepees, which could be easily transported. Although they relied primarily on hunting, they were close enough to the woodland environment to adopt some farming practices.

With the intrusion of Euro-Americans, the traditional skills of tribal members became obsolete. Successive land cessions meant that the Indians moved too often to settle into homes and raise crops, and their hunting grounds were shrinking. The Indians came to depend on the federal government for food and other supplies that were available at trading posts and white settlements. The string of trading posts and Indian agencies along the frontier accompanied the Indian removal acts. The federal government's policy was aimed at preserving and protecting Indian civilization by removing the native people from, and thus avoiding conflict with, Euro-Americans, with their vastly different cultural values and customs. Some politicians and liberal thinkers hoped

to save the Native American culture from destruction. In reality, the removal policy only contributed to the disintegration of Indian culture and almost destroyed an entire people. The Indians were moved from their rich native lands to Kansas, Oklahoma, and the Dakotas, a region most whites considered the Great American Desert.

In only one generation (1824–1851), Indian tribes ceded all the land within the boundaries of the state of Iowa in return for the equivalent of roughly 11 cents an acre from the federal government, which then offered the same land to land speculators and white settlers at an average price of $1.25 an acre. The Indians' inability to understand or cope with white culture and technology, along with their different concept of property ownership, left them without a homeland and with scarcely enough money to pay off the large debts they had incurred with local traders.

The persistence of the members of one tribe, the Mesquakie, and their refusal to abandon their homes in Iowa distinguish them from other North American tribes. A small band of eighty Mesquakie chose to remain in Iowa rather than move to Kansas with the rest of the tribe. In 1857 they arranged to purchase eighty acres of land in Tama County for a thousand dollars. By adhering to the legal and economic systems of whites, they were able to acquire their own land—not a government reservation— as a private enclave for bringing up future generations of their tribe. Although they struggled without government annuities for a decade and often suffered through hard winters and lean years, the Mesquakie managed to retain those parts of their culture most important to them. They continued to farm in the summer, trap and hunt on neighboring farmland, and trade goods for other necessities. The Mesquakie maintained a relatively primitive self-sufficiency, and social and religious customs remained much the same until after the turn of the century.

By 1900 the Mesquakie Settlement along the Iowa River had grown to almost 3,000 acres, with about 360 people in sixty-five households. After an outbreak of smallpox in 1901, the government forced the tribe to live apart rather than in a village setting, which created some divisiveness within the tribe. But they still held annual celebrations—called Corn Dances at harvesttime, a forerunner of the powwow still held each year. When Duren H. Ward visited the Mesquakie Settlement in 1905, under the auspices of the State Historical Society of Iowa, he found that life there was virtually unchanged. Most Mesquakie still lived in wickiups, though a few frame houses had been built. The government school and resident missionaries had little if any influence on life at the settlement. It was not until after the two world wars that significant changes in the living patterns of the tribe took place. The Mesquakie were successful in preserving their tribal heritage and cultural identity by staying close to their home in Iowa. The tribe was fortunate in avoiding the displacement and warfare that became the fate of other tribes, such as the Winnebago and the Sioux.

Agriculturalists and entrepreneurs were eager to settle "The Garden" as quickly as the Indians could be removed from the land. They were attracted by the cheap land, the fertile soil, and the ideal climate, with its abundant rainfall and long growing season. Natural waterways provided the necessary transportation routes to markets. Even before the surveyors finished their work, settlers were claiming the land, building crude shelters, and putting in their first crops. Most of these early pioneers acquired their land by purchase directly from the government or from land speculators. As guidebooks and pamphlets for immigrants extolling the virtues of the country were published and widely disseminated, the onrush of frontier settlers began.

The entire state was surveyed by 1858, laying out the land according to the federal grid of sections and townships. By 1860, parts of Iowa were well established and mature, while others were still on the edge of the frontier. New lands in the north central and western regions of the state were just opening up to settlement as transportation routes were established and the prairie sod broken. As the westward expansion of the nation proceeded, Iowa served as a crossroads and eventually a home, mainly for farmers but also for entrepreneurs, skilled and unskilled laborers, and their families.

Iowa's earliest pioneers came from New England, the mid-Atlantic states, the South, and the states of the old Northwest Territory. Along with this population of Americans there was an influx of foreign-born immigrants, primarily from western and northern Europe. The successive waves of immigration in the nineteenth century brought large numbers of people from the British Isles and Germany. Some communities and counties were heavily populated with clusters of Swedish, Norwegian, Danish, Dutch, and Czech settlers. Other nationalities like Canadians, Austrians, and French also immigrated to Iowa but not in such substantial numbers. In 1890 nearly one in five Iowans was foreign-born. After the turn of the century, other ethnic groups arrived from Italy, Greece, Poland, and Russia.

Small numbers of African-Americans came to Iowa from the surrounding states of Illinois and Missouri as well as from Kentucky, Tennessee, Virginia, Alabama, and Mississippi. By 1860 slightly over 1,000 blacks were concentrated in relatively few counties, most notably Lee County. Although their numbers had increased to 19,000 by 1920 with migration to such cities as Waterloo and Des Moines, blacks remained less than 1 percent of the total population. Coal-mining operations in Mahaska, Monroe, and Wapello and other counties accounted for the sizable numbers of blacks in these areas before 1910, but urban areas attracted greater numbers of blacks as the mines played out and new jobs in industry or in rail yards became available.

Each group brought its own customs and traditions, which gave each a distinctive cultural identity. Even with a degree of cultural assimilation, immigrants retained important elements of their native heritage, especially religious practices, ethnic celebrations, and family holidays. Despite ethnic differences and cultural barriers between groups, settlers who came to Iowa shared common assumptions. Attracted as they were to some of the most fertile land in the world, few had any qualms about displacing Native Americans, and most were willing to exploit the land for economic gain, even at the expense of the environment. Pioneers, who sometimes encountered rich prairie topsoil almost two feet deep, commonly thought the black soil was so thick it would last forever. But once the land was plowed and farmed year after year, the topsoil rapidly began to wash away with the rain and blow away with the wind, leaving less than eight inches of the precious topsoil in many places today.

We were once a powerful, but now a small nation. When the white people first crossed the big water and landed on this island, they were then small as we now are.

—Speech by Mesquakie Chief Wapello at treaty talks on October 16, 1841, Letters Received by the Office of Indian Affairs

Nag-ga-rash, "Head Chief" of the Iowa tribe, after whom the state was named, 1860s. The original is a carte de visite.

(Frank) Sha-wa-ta, born in 1874 (left), and Mu-kwa-pa-na-sha (Young Bear), born in 1867. 17 × 14 glass plate negative, Ward Collection.

This is all the country we have left; and we are so few now we cannot conquer other countries. You now see me, and all my people. Have pity on us, we are but few, and are fast melting away.

—Chief Wapello, October 16, 1841

An unidentified
Mesquakie woman.
4½ × 3¼ glass
plate negative.

Kwi-ya-ma,
born in 1833.
5 × 3¼ glass plate
negative, Ward
Collection.

Summer shade, Mesquakie Settlement, ca. 1905. At far left is She-ske-que. 5 × 7, Ward Collection.

From their own savings [the Foxes] bought about 1,300 acres of land, which they now occupy and pay taxes on like other people, and it is their own as completely as any farm in the state belongs to any person, although, for prudential reasons, the title instead of resting in the tribe or its chief, is deeded to the governor of Iowa, to hold in trust for them. The Foxes now receive as their income annually, as above mentioned, about $22,000. This tribe has for many censuses remained about the same, numerically—from 360 to 365; the last was 362. There are no Sac Indians in Iowa. That name is pronounced Sauk.

—Cedar Rapids *Evening Gazette*, May 15, 1889, p. 2

Chi-na-ha's (Jennie Davenport's) wick-iup, Mesquakie Settlement, Tama County, ca. 1900–1905. This is more like a lodge house.

"Meskwaki scene."
6 × 8.

This land is all we have; it is our only fortune. When it is gone, we shall have nothing left.
—Chief Wapello, October 16, 1841

Boys on ponies,
Mesquakie Settle-
ment, ca. 1905.
6 × 8.

Two Mesquakie girls posed with two white girls in Tama. H. C. Eberhart, photographer; 6½ × 4⅛.

*Group portrait of
the students who
came from various
clans to the Toledo
school, August
1899. $4\frac{1}{2} \times 6\frac{1}{2}$.*

*A Mesquakie
woman in a camp
near Amana, ca.
1893. H. Roy Mos-
nat, photographer;
4 × 5.*

Ki-wa-si-qua (Elsie Morgan), Mesquakie Settlement, Tama County, ca. 1915–1920. She was the wife of John Buffalo. Edward Rosheim Collection.

Weaving at George Soldier's wickiup, Mesquakie Settlement, Tama County, ca. 1915. C. W. Wright, photographer; 3½ × 5 postcard.

A powwow at the Mesquakie Settlement, ca. 1915–1920. Svacina Collection.

[In 1902] two Winnebagos came to visit the Mesquakie. With them came smallpox. The settlement was quarantined for six months. Forty-three Mesquakie died that year. . . . Next the government forced the tribe to live apart and not in a village setting. That I think got rid of the village and tribal spirit of the Mesquakie. Then the tribe started to fight among themselves, because they did not have village rules anymore. Sure, people lived apart during winter hunts and trappings, but they always had a village to come home to.

—Oral history interview with Adeline Wanatee at the Mesquakie Settlement, conducted by Johnathan Buffalo in March 1977

This land is held in common in the name of the tribe, this being the only tribe that owns its own land by right of purchase and pays taxes on it the same as any white owner.

In the early days of Tama County, the tribe suffered in various ways, from lack of food, from exposure, from disease and epidemics. Then later, they suffered appreciably during the period of transition from the wicki-up mode of living to the white man's frame house, because of lack of knowledge of sanitary measures.

—George Youngbear in a booklet printed by the Mesquakie United Presbyterian Church, ca. 1970

18   Indians and the Land

*The Sixth Iowa
Cavalry camped at
its headquarters in
Dakota Territory in
1862. This unit
helped build Fort
Sully and was in-
volved in military
action against the
Sioux Indians.
1863. 4 × 5½.*

Probably nine-tenths of the eastern, and a still larger proportion of the western half of the State of Iowa is prairie. The timber is in general found skirting the streams, while the prairie occupies the whole of the higher portion of the country, with the exception of here and there an isolated group of trees standing like an island amid ocean. . . .

In ascending from the level of a river to the high land in its vicinity, we first cross the "bottom land," or "bottom," the portion of the valley which is level and but little elevated above the surface of the stream. These bottom lands are frequently heavily timbered and with a great variety of trees, among which the elm, linden, black walnut, white and burr oak, poplar and ash are the most common. . . . Generally the width of the valley is proportioned to the size of the stream; so that on small tributaries there is but a narrow belt of low land, within which the stream meanders with a very crooked course, crossing and re-crossing from one side of the valley to the other.

—*Handbook and Guide to 1,200,000 Acres of Iowa Land in the Middle Region of Western Iowa*, published by the Iowa Railroad Land Company in 1878, p. 4

"Streams in Iowa flowed in all directions before they were straightened," north of Ames, ca. 1900. 5 × 7, courtesy Mrs. A. P. Kehlenbeck.

The Middle Region of Western Iowa presents attractions for the farmer which, taken as a whole, cannot be surpassed by any portion of the United States. Undulating prairies, interspersed with open groves of timber, and watered by streams pure and transparent, hills of moderate height and gentle slope—these are the ordinary features of the pastoral landscape. No country is more fertile, nor does any afford greater facilities for bringing wild lands under cultivation. Its native prairies are fields almost ready made to the hands of the tiller. . . . Its broad fields, unbroken by stumps or other obstructions, afford the finest scope for the mower, the reaper, the planter, and other agricultural implements which have been invented to save the labor of the husbandman.

—Iowa Railroad Land Company's *Handbook and Guide*, p. 6

Surveyors.
7½ × 9½,
State Historical
Society of Iowa,
Des Moines.

CHAPTER 2 : THE COUNTRYSIDE

The settlement of the Iowa countryside may be seen as the culmination of an agrarian philosophy that dominated American life for over two hundred years, one which emphasized the democratic ideal: political and economic strength through those who worked the land. In short, Iowa is the quintessential agricultural state. Like other midwestern states, it was settled by people seeking a Garden of Eden that would provide economic stability and prosperity in a peaceful pastoral setting. Agricultural techniques, already mastered through successive generations of farming, were modified when settlers reached the prairies of the American West. New technological innovations such as the steel moldboard plow, the reaper, the riding cultivator, the steam thresher, and the gasoline tractor eased the labor of farming and stimulated further improvements. The spirit of the independent farmer, combined with an ideal crop-growing environment and rapidly expanding transportation system to carry crops to market, soon placed Iowa among the leading agricultural states in the nation. During most of the period between 1860 and 1920, the Iowa farmer continued to believe in progress and prosperity despite repeated periods of economic uncertainty.

Iowa was settled over a period of less than forty years. While the wilderness offered favorable climatic conditions, well-watered land, and a thick layer of black topsoil, the landscape had to be altered to fit the farmers' needs. Homesteaders erected shelters, built fences, and improved the land for farming by breaking the tough prairie sod, with its mass of intertwined roots, and tiling and draining swampy areas and sloughs. They also built bridges over rivers and creeks and laid out roads to market. On the frontier, farmers were concerned with providing for the immediate needs of their families. Ever more land was put into production, and the commercial market for farm products became firmly established.

Farm activities naturally followed seasonal rhythms—planting in the spring, cultivating and haying through the summer, and harvesting and threshing in the fall. Both men and women played important roles in the operation of the family farm, working from dawn to dusk. Fathers and sons plowed fields, raised barns, and sawed wood,

"Our cows," near Lost Island Lake, Ruthven, ca. 1912–1917. E. M. Clark photographer; 3½

while mothers and daughters tended gardens, helped with fieldwork when necessary, and performed endless household duties, including the preparation of meals for both family and farm help. Tending livestock, including milking cows twice daily, required considerable energy and time. Children were recruited to help with farm chores at an early age.

Horses provided the main source of power for farm machinery, as well as for transportation. Thus the care and feeding of these animals were essential tasks in the everyday life of the farm. Someone had to rise early to feed the animals, prepare the harnesses, curry and brush the horses, or clean out the barn. The most powerful draft horses, such as Percherons, Belgians, and Clydesdales, were imported from Europe and used to improve a farmer's stock.

Finding themselves far from urban amenities, homesteaders specialized in self-sufficiency in order to stock their cupboards. They planted orchards and gardens, gathered honey and made maple syrup, raised hogs and sheep, and bred horses and livestock. Farm wives were experts at preserving fruits and vegetables, and raising poultry for meat and eggs was one of their prime activities. The huckster's wagon from town came around to deliver groceries or trade for eggs and produce. Cooler weather from late fall to early spring offered the perfect time for hog butchering on the farm. Afterward, the meat was salted and smoked or made into sausage. Family members also hunted, bringing home fresh venison, prairie chickens, and rabbits for the dinner table.

Farmsteads were clusters of buildings, each designed and built for a specific function. Besides the main barn, the assortment of outbuildings to be found on an Iowa farm might include a dairy barn and milk house, chicken coops, hog houses, and one or more corncribs or storage bins. Many farm households also had a summer kitchen, a smokehouse, a woodshed, and an outhouse. Scraps of lumber were saved in the barn, waiting for the next building project or for the day when someone could drive out the old nails and straighten them.

Some farmers recognized the wisdom of planting a windbreak of trees, both for the sheer beauty of the trees and for protection from the strong prairie winds or drifting snow. A stand of trees on a farmer's property provided the comforts of summer shade, the necessary fuel for wood-burning stoves, and construction materials for various projects around the farm. The farmer with excess timber might secure a modest profit by selling wood to less-fortunate neighbors. Corncobs were also a common source of fuel for heating homes, cooking, or even smoking meat.

A successful farm often depended on the availability of water from a nearby stream or creek. With more advanced technology, wells could be drilled, not just dug, and windmills could be erected to pump water both for livestock and for household use.

Windmills appeared as a dominant feature on the horizon, varying from the intricate wooden slats arranged in a fan to the more common steel windmill like the Aeromotor. Later, windmills were used for generating electricity on the farm, with excess current stored in battery cells for future use.

If farm families prospered, they added to existing structures or simply tore down old buildings and built new. Sizable families and extra farm help meant that large households were common. Many older homesteads were replaced by modern two-story farmhouses when the electrification and mechanization of the household eventually reached the countryside. Indoor plumbing eliminated chores like hauling and heating water, while other modern conveniences such as coal furnaces made homes more comfortable. Technological changes came as late as the 1920s, the 1930s, or even the 1940s to some households, affecting daily life on the farm in far-reaching ways.

Since not everyone was able to purchase or inherit their own farmland, some farmers had to rent the land or work it for a relative. March was the traditional month for tenant farmers to establish themselves for the season, moving into a house that often needed repair and starting the spring fieldwork. Although family members were the cheapest laborers, people outside the family might help with farm chores. Hired hands and itinerant laborers were common, especially during the summer months, and neighbors would also pitch in when necessary. The hired hand or hired girl, who worked in return for room and board and small wages, offered critical support on the farm, performing heavy labor or household tasks.

Community spirit and neighborly cooperation were essential ingredients in any rural area. A day's work on a neighbor's farm was considered a fair trade for future assistance, and people were careful to stay square with their neighbors. This cooperation was perhaps best exemplified during harvesttime, when able-bodied neighbors would assist with the cutting and stacking of grain. There was a shared sense of responsibility, for everyone knew that hay and grain crops needed to be harvested quickly and at just the right time. In the post–Civil War years, thousands of seasonal laborers descended on Iowa's wheat fields, moving from farm to farm.

Threshing (or thrashing, as some said) was an annual event, mixing communal excitement with hard but rewarding work. The threshing ring made the rounds of each farm in the neighborhood, and farmers made detailed arrangements as soon as the order of work was decided. Nearly everyone, including children, was involved in preparing for the big day at their farm. Since most farmers had only enough water stored for the workhorses to drink, extra water was brought in wagons for the steam-powered engines that powered the grain separators. Each person on the threshing ring was assigned a specific duty, with some people performing more disagreeable jobs than others. The farm wives, farmers' daughters, and hired girls were busy in the kitchen preparing the meal for the hungry and thirsty crew, who might eat in shifts.

The development of new machinery and improved methods helped to ameliorate some of the most difficult aspects of farm life. The Harvestor-Thresher, invented in 1888, was a great improvement over the old reapers. Later, in the twentieth century, the tractor would revolutionize farm labor, but horses were continually used well into the 1930s. This mechanization influenced Iowa farmers in a profound way, as did the spread of so-called book farming. Farm practices in the nineteenth century were based on traditional wisdom, passed on largely through hands-on experience. But even before the 1860s, some Iowans were keenly aware of the need for careful, scientific farming. Agricultural reformers believed that better farming practices would not only increase yields and production but would also help to save the land for future generations of farmers.

As early as the 1850s, Iowa farmers formed agricultural societies to help spread knowledge about proven farming practices. County and state fairs provided a forum for exchanging ideas and for exhibiting the best products. A land grant from the federal government made possible the establishment of the Iowa State Agricultural College in Ames, and the first students enrolled in 1868. Farm-bred youth studied agricultural science, which included conservation practices such as crop rotation, sound business and farm management methods, and the significance of careful plant and animal breeding.

The development and proliferation of farm journals also greatly contributed to the increased awareness of the average farmer. *The Iowa Homestead, Wallaces' Farmer*, and *Successful Farming* were just a few of the farm journals. In 1900, at the beginning of the golden age of Iowa agriculture, the Iowa Department of Agriculture was established. Among other programs, it began publishing the *Year Book of Agriculture*, which provided indispensable information to many farmers. Iowa State College created an extension department in 1906 and in 1912 employed a network of county agents, who conducted demonstrations and explained to farmers that the "new" agriculture involved business management.

Throughout this time Iowa farmers were involved in a wide range of issues affecting the rural community. The question of transportation, however, overshadowed nearly all of the farmers' concerns, since they needed to be able to transport their surplus to markets both in this country and throughout the world. Because they depended on adequate and economical transportation, the fairness of railroad rates remained a central issue in Iowa politics for decades. There were also other important matters, such as the control of financial capital by bankers, so farmers sought ways to discuss their problems and to search for effective solutions. The nonpartisan Granger movement, which reached 100,000 members in 1875, is one example of the social and political organizations that were formed. Farmers' clubs were organized into the Farmers' Alliance, which worked for legislative changes and helped spawn the Populist party. Farmers also banded together in cooperatives or in associations such as the Live Stock Shippers Association or the Farmers Grain Dealers Association. Farmers were attempting to make their voices heard as a group in the expanding national economic and political scene. By the late teens, the National Farmers' Union and the Iowa Farm Bureau had emerged to play leading roles in farm politics.

At first, farmers depended on local markets to sell their products and to purchase those items they could not produce themselves. During the early years of farming in Iowa, the local mill was an important outlet for their wheat crop. Usually located on a river or stream, the mill utilized grindstones and later rollers to produce a fine flour for sale in local and regional markets. In pioneer days, the farmers' very survival rested on the existence of a nearby mill, but improved transportation created by the railroads fostered the development of large companies in cities, and local millers eventually went out of business.

Early Iowa farmers produced wheat as their main crop, but increased production in other newly settled states, combined with natural forces such as soil depletion, grasshoppers, and chinch bugs, made it infeasible to rely on a one-crop system. By the 1870s farmers were being forced to adapt and diversify their operations to be successful. This change led to increased specialization and the switch to more dairy farming, along with raising beef cattle, hogs, and other livestock. Farmers tended crops of wheat, oats, barley, timothy, clover, and later alfalfa. Corn, however, became the staple crop in Iowa, because it allowed farmers to fatten their livestock for sale to meat packers in the local area and later in markets farther east. This shift to selling livestock necessitated new markets for Iowa products, thereby transforming and expanding the farm economy. The feeder cattle and hog business required a considerable outlay of capital, and many farmers found it impossible to invest large sums of money. Instead, small-scale farmers might sell their surplus corn to neighbors with larger herds.

Just as a nearby mill had been essential to early wheat farmers, the grain elevator served as an important marketing outlet for the corn grower. Most farmers raised at least a few milk cows, and as they acquired larger herds the creamery became another vital business. The development of the cream separator in 1880 expanded Iowa's already booming butter production, making butter one of the state's leading exports.

Of course, other business enterprises were also crucial to the success of the family farm, but in general, farmers attempted to rely on their own skills to survive. In response to the needs of the surrounding rural population, towns and villages sprang up all over the state. Speculators and railroad companies laid out settlement tracts in advance of settlement. Railroad lines spread in every direction, creating a transportation network to regional and national markets. Nearly everyone was involved in the promotion of the state as a model of successful farming. Agriculture laid the foundation for Iowa's early industrial growth, which in turn enabled some towns to grow into larger metropolitan centers. Complex relationships and mutual support systems arose between rural and urban areas, but the groups depended on one another and were dedicated to and connected with the prime force supporting the state's economy—farming.

Ole Thorson clearing a twenty-acre field with the help of Osvald Ugland and Lars Reierson, Elgin, 1912.
3½ × 4½.

A bird's-eye view of Clermont, ca. 1910. 3¼ × 5½.

The Olund family
farm in northwest
Iowa, ca. 1891–
1895. 8 × 10.

A farmer with a
cultivator.

The Bonnell broth-
ers' barn five miles
north of Donnell-
son. It was built in
the mid 1840s.

April 30, 1878
Am now done planting corn, nearly 40 acres, and presume it will be many years before I can make a similar record.
—Diary of Alfred T. Giauque of Van Buren County

May 22, 1878
Replant Corn. Very much missed owing to worms and mice, and mice still working on it. Very discouraging.
—Diary of Alfred T. Giauque of Van Buren County

The prairies are never perfectly level, there are almost imperceptible gradations in the surface which lead the eye on and on to where some farmstead with its grove marks the horizon.
—"Corn," by Hortense Butler Heywood of Peterson, ca. 1910–1915

April 21, 1883

M. Fisher and the hired men are up at the R.R. crossing unloading the cars of lumber for new barns.

—Diary of Mary Fisher of Butler County

The frame of a new barn near West Liberty, ca. 1905. W. A. Warren, photographer; 5 × 7 glass plate negative, W. A. Warren Collection.

Building a barn near McGregor, ca. 1910. Duluth Pieper, photographer; 4 × 5 glass plate negative, Duluth Pieper Collection.

With the help of the farmer it took about one day to assemble and erect a windmill. . . . The legs were placed about 5 feet below ground level and bolted to a plate of iron at ground level. Another alternative was to place the legs in cement if the farmer had no intention of moving the windmill. The height of the windmill determined the amount of taper of the legs. Heights ranged from 30 to 70 feet, depending on the needs of the farmer.

—Interview with Fred H. Takes of Bernard in November 1980

Raising a windmill in Ida County, possibly on the Warren Neal farm in the 1890s. Note the hand-built wooden tower. 4 × 5 glass plate negative, original owned by Michael Mendellson.

A farmyard scene with a boy on a horse, possibly in Johnson County, ca. 1900. 7¾ × 9¾, Pratt Collection.

A family at a corn-crib in the 1870s. 6½ × 9½, original mounted on cloth.

[In about 1913] they put a generating plant in the basement with a lot of batteries. You would crank this motor up to charge up the batteries. The batteries would be what would light up things, and we even had a light up in the haymow. Was just a little light, but you didn't need but just a little light. Would be better than a lantern. You would turn it on at the bottom, you know, and you would go up there and pitch your hay down.

—Oral history interview with Clark Brindle of Conrad, conducted by Roger Raum on March 27, 1977

A house, with a sleigh at the right, near West Liberty, ca. 1904. W. A. Warren, photographer; 5 × 7 glass plate negative, W. A. Warren Collection.

A barn near West Liberty, ca. 1904. W. A. Warren, photographer; 5 × 7 glass plate negative, W. A. Warren Collection.

One day the whole neighborhood is as permanent, as settled, as stable as if it were to exist thus for years to come. The next the roads are filled with a unique procession—farm wagons piled high with household goods and trailing behind their corn plows, seeders, and other pieces of machinery, loads of grain wherein the clever housewife has packed her precious fruit jars, loads of squealing hogs, small herds of restless, frightened cattle, all of which the farmer like the patriarchs of old moves from the place which he has called home for the past year to the place which he will call home for the coming year.

—"The First of March," by Hortense Butler Heywood of Peterson, ca. 1910–1915

A farmstead with family members, horses, and a carriage on the front lawn in the 1890s. 6 × 8.

Cloverdale Farm, the home of Rev. A. Jacobson, near Decorah, ca. 1910. The farm was established by his father, Jacob Abrahamson. 3¼ × 5½.

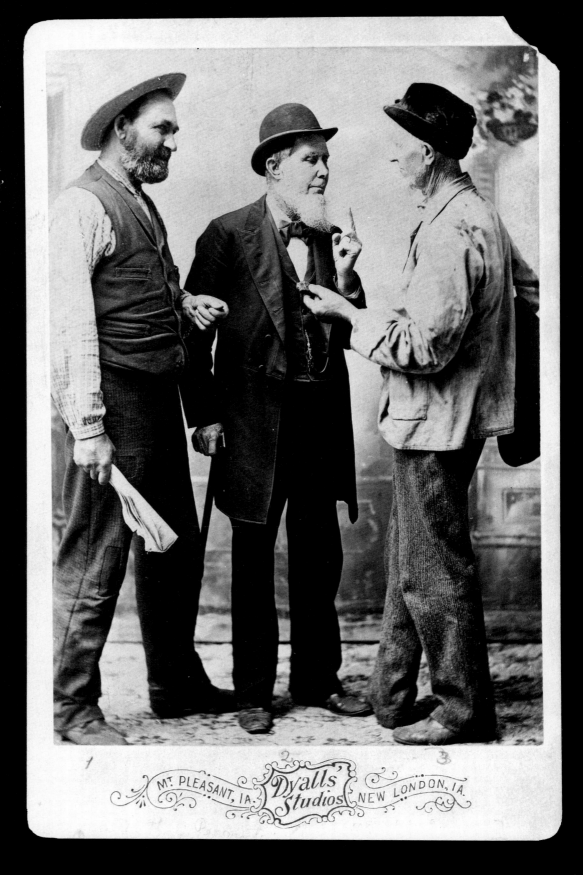

"Three prominent Henry County farmers in a humorous mood." From left: "James L. Portlock, J. Dovermann, Lew Davey offering a 'chaw' of plug tobacco." New London, 1890s. Dyalls' Studios, photographer; 5⅛ × 4.

A demonstration of the "Avery tractor" in Mills County, ca. 1910. This is believed to have been the first tractor in Mills County. 5½ × 6½, Allen Wortman Collection.

Of course, one farmer can now farm a half section with a tractor, or even more. In those days, it took so much time, and then if you had a lot of livestock, you had a full-time job from early morning to late at night. Pull that leather on and off those horses, clean the barn, and roll the hay down out of the mow, and clean the barn, and haul the manure out, and hitch 'em up and feed them, and pull that leather. Boy, we done a lot of that. About all you could plow was about five acres a day with a five- or six-horse team.

Just a one-bottom plow?

No, two-bottom. Two fourteen-inch. And you didn't get your stalks disked up very good. You would ride the plow, and you could kick the stalks down between the moldboards so that instead of balling up all the time, they would go right through and you wouldn't have to stop.

—Oral history interview with Clark Brindle of Conrad, conducted by Roger Raum on March 27, 1977

"Seed Corn Gospel Train," 1905. Perry G. Holden of the Iowa State Agricultural College traveled to all corners of the state to spread the word about improved seed corn. Iowa State University Archives.

Laying drainage tiles, Boone County, ca. 1914. Kock Collection.

Most heavy soils are much improved by draining; open drains to carry off the surface-water, and covered drains, that which settles beneath. An acquaintance covered a low, wet, clayey field with a net-work of under drains, and from a production of almost nothing but grass, it yielded the first year forty bushels of wheat per acre, enough to pay the expense, and admitted of much easier tillage afterwards.

—*The North-Western Review*, June 1857, p. 16

Jim Burgoin operating a binder, Silver City, ca. 1900. G. A. Spellbring, photographer; Allen Wortman Collection.

Three women and a boy with shocks of grain, ca. 1900. 4 × 4¾, Irish Collection.

Fresh manure is generally in a state not readily mixed with soils. It is thrown into large lumps over the surface, some of which are ploughed in, and others not; but none of them prove of immediate use to the crops. But, on the other hand, fermented manure, from its ready pulverization, admits of easy admixture. Let fresh manure be thoroughly ground down, and worked into the soil by repeated harrowings, and two or three ploughings, and its influence will be like magic.

—*The North-Western Review*, June 1857, p. 19

"Fertilizing the fields." Spreading manure on the F. W. Reasoner farm, Pine Lawn, near Humboldt, ca. 1900. 2 × 2¾, courtesy Arlene R. Sayre.

*A four-horse team
pulling a harvester,
ca. 1905–1910. 3½
× 5½ postcard.*

Father used to take us children with him on all occasions. He liked children, it was a help to Mother to take us with him, and when big enough we could do all kinds of errands for him, if only to hold a tool until he wanted it, or to empty the heavy milk pails into the big cans on the bench in the cow stable. Also he liked us to follow the plow or the mower in case he wanted anything done—many miles for short legs! But there were compensations. If we followed the plow, the cool, moist earth felt good to bare feet, meadow larks and quail flew from cover, and a mowing machine brought down wonderful bunches of red clover and brown-eyed Susans to take home to Mother.

—"Evergreens and Our Family Circle," a reminiscence by Edith Mather of Cedar
   County, ca. 1939, p. 11

A threshing crew, Communia, 1888. 5¼ × 7½, George Muegge Collection.

A threshing crew at the Kessler farm, possibly in Johnson County, in the 1880s. This early steam-engine thresher was not self-propelled but had to be pulled by horses.

We thrashed with steam in those days. Now, when I say steam I mean the thrashing separator was pulled by a steam engine. People see those today and think what a monstrosity those were. Well, they had to be big because, remember, they had a boiler. And you had to build a fire in them in the firebox. And, really, a steam engine was composed of a one-cylinder steam engine mounted on top of the boiler with a governor on it and with the black smoke puffing out of the smokestack, in a pop-off valve, releasing steam occasionally. It did look like a monster. We could usually thrash, oh, perhaps forty acres a day.

The separator and the steam engine, of course, they set stationary. And the bundles had to be hauled in by hayrack and unloaded into this machine, and, of course, we had to have grain wagons to haul the thrashed grain away. Now, the thrashed straw was going out by a straw stack. We had stackers that stacked the straw, but I'm telling you that was a dusty job. Sometimes a farmer would have this straw loaded into his barn. That made it convenient in the wintertime, when he used it for bedding. He didn't have to dig it out of the snow.

—Oral history interview with Harold Donham of Iowa City, conducted by Alvin
  Schroeder on March 27, 1977

Machine at I. Newton's place Sep. 1894

A threshing crew at
I. Newton's place,
September 1894.
The original is
color-tinted, with a
convex surface.
18 × 20.

A threshing rig near Wellman in 1912. 3 × 5¼.

Four harvesters resting in a field. 3½ × 5½ postcard.

"When will the threshers get to our place?" The answer was always uncertain, depending on the weather and how often the machine broke down. There were times when there was only an afternoon's warning before supper had to be ready for 15 hungry men.

—"Women's Role in Threshing," by Ruth Sayre, in *Threshing Days on an Iowa Farm* (Des Moines: Living History Farms, 1977)

Before the men came in for dinner, one of the kitchen crew hung a mirror on a tree in the yard and beneath it put a basin on a bench with a pail of water, soap, and towel and comb so that the men could wash up.

Most farm dinner tables could not serve the whole threshing crew at one time, so the first table was cleared, the dishes washed and reset with much hurrying and scurrying about of the women.

—"Women's Role in Threshing," by Ruth Sayre

There were big platters of roast beef, platters of fried chicken, big bowls of mashed potatoes, of riced potatoes, and gallons of gravy. And of course, every housewife, you know, in this contest they would have, they would have special, exotic dishes that we didn't know what they were, but they were good. And there was gallons of iced tea and coffee, topped by pies—apple pie, cherry pie, chocolate pies—chocolate cakes. You name it, they had it.

—Oral history interview with Harold Donham of Iowa City, conducted by Alvin Schroeder on March 21, 1977

We had helped to get the ground ready for corn. When we got that done, then we'd have to cultivate. Of course, we had seeded the oats before, and we cultivated corn three times or four with a single-row cultivator. . . . That would take me four months, the first of June up until the end of July to get the corn laid by, and then we would have some hay to make, and as soon as the hay was taken care of, we started planting some oats.

We would tie the oats into bundles and each bundle was probably two feet around, or three feet, and they would carry those on up and drop them off in windrows, and you would pick them up out of this windrow and take them in a shock, nine bundles in a shock, you would put eight in and then put a cap on it to keep it draining so it would drain and dry out alright.

—Oral history interview with Charlie Summerson of Dawson,
    conducted by Mary Bennett on April 8, 1977

"Lunch in the field." Shown are Christian, Elisabeth, Hulda (girl at left), Jacob, Lydia, and William Gabelmann. Karl Walther or Bertha Gabelmann, photographer; Gabelmann Collection.

A full load of hay, with reaper in the background, Shenandoah, 1911. 3½ × 5 postcard, Alma Fallers Collection.

"Putting the hay in the barn on the Sven Blockhus farm," Elgin, 1910. "A huge fork was pushed down into the load of loose hay. A heavy rope was locked to this fork, and was strung along the top by the means of several pullies. The team on the right was hitched to the other end of the rope and pulled hay up."

*Loading a hayrack
in Clayton County.
4 × 3.*

*Haystacks on the
Roslien family
farm, Kensett,
ca. 1900–1910.*

*4 × 4¾ glass plate
negative, Nels L.
Roslien Collection.*

[Hay loaders] would be fastened on behind a wagon hayrack, and as the horses
walked, the load[er] would lift the hay from the ground and put it on the wagon.
—"Life on the Farm," a reminiscence by Leonard B. Jaques of Greene County, 1973

Pulling ears one at a time and on frosty mornings when the air was still, one could tell how many of his neighbors was out and what time they got out in the field. All you had to do was stop and listen and you could hear this bang, bang, bang. You could hear it to the north, south, the east, and to the west of you.

. . . Of course, sometimes it was a family thing, picking corn. And this community we lived in, the boys and the girls and even the housewife would go out and pick corn. But in my situation, Dad and me picked it, and oftentimes, when our neighbors had the corn out, we would hire neighbor boys. We usually paid them enough if I remember right, around four cents per bushel. And so, if one could pick a hundred bushel a day, he made four dollars a day.

. . . Most people used either a hook or a peg. Now, a peg was just a thing, a little farm implement that . . . one fits over his fingers on his right hand. . . . The husk was pulled loose, you slid the hand up on the underside and give the ear a twist, and in one motion you threw it in the wagon. Some people used . . . palm hooks and wrist hooks. As they reached for the ear, they would reach past it and drag the arm or the hand past the ear, catching the husk, pulling them loose, and as the husk was pulled loose, they grabbed the ear, give it a twist, and tossed it in the wagon.

We used mittens, of course, what they called husking mittens. . . . Our fingers would be sore, and on frosty mornings and on days it was snowing, the mittens would get wet, our hands would get chapped, and sometimes we'd leave blood drops on the snow.

—Oral history interview with Harold Donham of Iowa City, conducted by Alvin Schroeder on March 21, 1977

Well, the corn, we harvested that by hand. Had a bangboard on the other side of usually a triple-box wagon, probably 10 foot long and about 3 foot deep and about 3 foot wide. And that would hold a bushel to the inch of ear corn. And when it was full, that was 36 inches or thereabouts. And the real good picker could ordinarily get about 50 bushels in a half a day after he got toughened into it. It usually took most of two weeks to get toughened into it for most people. . . . But then after that, you could get up early and pick about 100 bushels every day. I have picked a lot more than that. I have picked 153 bushels in one day, and that's a lot. I mean, some men I have heard that could pick almost 200 bushels a day. That's really moving.

—Oral history interview with Clark Brindle of Conrad, conducted by Roger Raum on March 27, 1977

Elevating corn at the William Starr farm in Wright County. 3¾ × 4¾, Klassie Collection.

Making silage to store in the silo at the left. Note the mud and straw on the wagon wheels. Karl Walther or Bertha Gabelmann, photographer; Gabelmann Collection.

Grinding sorghum with a horse-powered grinder, Iowa Falls, ca. 1890. 3¾ × 5.

In the fall at sugarcane cutting time, we would stop at the Schooley sorghum mills. The juice was boiled in huge flat pans. We were given a dish and spoon to sample this lovely warm buttery molasses, to our great delight. Mother kept a big sorghum jug for breakfast buckwheats, but it never equalled that, fresh and warm at the mill.
—"Sweets," a reminiscence by Edith Mather of Cedar County, ca. 1939, p. 1

The long high corn crib stood in the orchard to the north. For many years it was Jeanne's and my duty to feed the hogs from here at night after school. This meant the hogs knew feeding time and what our appearance meant, and, as many of the old hogs were rather cross, we felt it was a race for life to run ahead of the swarming and squealing hogs and scramble up the steep sides of the crib before they'd catch our legs, as we thought. When this pig-hungry-cry was taken up, pigs feeding in distant corners would come running along the smart-weed-lined paths at a smart pig-gallop. Boards were taken off the crib sides according to the fullness of the crib, although when the supply was low, we had to throw three, four, or seven hundred ears high up over these boards. The hogs were greedy, noisy feeders and never gave us any notice as we climbed down, and as this was usually one of the last chores, we were glad enough to hurry in for our own supper.

—"Evergreens and Our Family Circle," by Edith Mather, p. 7

*Hogs on a fence,
near McGregor, ca.
1910. Duluth Pie-
per, photographer;
4¾ × 4 glass plate
negative, Duluth
Pieper Collection.*

Hog butchering on the Gabelmann farm near Clarksville, ca. 1920. These men, using a pulley attached to a tree, are suspending the hog over a barrel of boiling water. Jacob Gabelmann is butchering the hog with the assistance of Tom Arjes. Karl Walther or Bertha Gabelmann, photographer; Gabelmann Collection.

Hog butchering, ca. 1913. The hair of the hog was scraped off after the hog was removed from the barrel of boiling water. The entrails of the animal were removed, and then the carcass was prepared for butchering. The original is a postcard.

When father unhitched the horses, the children, always under foot, were given the privilege of riding the harnessed horses "to drink," and into the barn. Each horse knew its own stall and needed no guiding.

—"Evergreens and Our Family Circle," by Edith Mather, pp. 7–8

Draft horses sold to George Wilcox on the S. F. Van farm, Griswold, February 11, 1913. Haldeman, photographer; 8 × 10.

Georgia Halvorson and her cow in front of her house in Story City. 5 × 8.

Mr. Flowers with his calves near McGregor. Duluth Pieper, photographer; 4 × 5 glass plate negative, Duluth Pieper Collection.

A man shearing sheep, Iowa Falls, ca. 1900. Frank E. Foster, photographer; 5 × 4 glass plate negative, Frank E. Foster Collection.

June 3, 1878

Go to Bonaparte with wool sell 52 lbs. off 12 sheep purchased for $17.50 and kept two fleeces for stocking yarn. Had an increase of 9 lambs and lost one old sheep to death. Wool sold amounts to $11.45.

—Diary of Alfred T. Giauque of Van Buren County

A little about my father in hiring help. . . . He would furnish . . . the house, a cow for milk, . . . some chickens for eggs, and also some young ones for frying. A rig, which was a team and buggy for grocer[y] buying and church, etc., plus $25 per month. . . . My father furnished a hog to butcher to a married man.

Single men received board, room, washing done, a house kept if they had one, or if they didn't, he would furnish one and $20 a month. In case a man quit it didn't take long to find another.

—"Life on the Farm," by Leonard B. Jaques

A woman tending her garden, ca. 1900. 3½ × 2½ postcard.

Tapping the wine barrel, Gabelmann farm, Clarksville, ca. 1920. Karl Walther or Bertha Gabelmann, photographer; Gabelmann Collection.

W. S. Furnace Poultry Yards, Lisbon, ca. 1880–1895. Jacoby and Barnes, photographer; 4¾ × 7½.

"The Mud Hen Flyer," a Rock Island Railroad car, ca. 1910–1915.

Loading cabbage from the J. W. Rummell farm onto railroad cars, Nichols, July 12, 1916.

[Charles H. Clark] operated his own shop and produced all of his own supplies of hives and equipment, of the wax and combs. He advertised and sold all apiary supplies, including comb foundation. Pure Italian queens and Pure Italian Bees a Speciality. . . .

This was his customary way, and mode in dress, when handling his bees. Unprotected face and hands, and a very little smoke was used. His motto was "Know your bees."

—Reverse side of the photograph of Clark and his daughter

Charles H. Clark and his daughter, Lilla, at his Plum Grove Apiary Farm in Monroe County, June 28, 1899.
4 × 2.

"Spraying apparatus." A man spraying an orchard from a horse-drawn water wagon, ca. 1910. 2 × 4.

A man beside a wagonload of apples, ca. 1910.
2 × 4.

A huckster wagon at the Lenoch farm, North Liberty, ca. 1910. Bert Bane was driving H. A. White's huckster wagon, which traveled around to buy eggs and butter and to deliver groceries. Jessie White Anderson Collection.

Wagons loaded with milk cans at the creamery in Troy Mills.

Farmers delivering shelled corn to a grain elevator in Corwith in 1913. Oxley, photographer; 3 1/2 × 5 postcard.

CHAPTER 3 : BUILDING MAIN STREET

As the settlement of Iowa's farmland progressed, the patterns of town life were also being established. Iowa's towns and cities were similar to other midwestern urban communities in that most were influenced by their rural surroundings. Many of the same values and attitudes associated with country life were also present in the towns. Arising simultaneously with farm settlement, Main Street was built primarily to serve as a marketing and business center for local farmers. Towns also provided a place for some degree of cultural and social activity, but the first priority of frontier settlers was to establish a viable economic base for town growth and stability.

Town builders realized that commercial and industrial development was essential if a town was to flourish and survive. The flow of settlement to a particular locality depended on accessible transportation routes and facilities, potential markets for goods, the quality of the surrounding land, and location in relation to other settlements. Early Iowa towns were founded along rivers—the Mississippi, Missouri, Des Moines, Cedar, and Iowa. Later, towns vied for the establishment of a railroad line, which could provide a direct link to larger markets. Elaborate schemes were played out, with sealed bids, extensive gifts of land to railroads, and countless political promises, all designed to secure a railroad and thereby insure a profitable future for the town. Railroad companies founded many of the small towns along their routes. In 1867 the Chicago and North Western became the first railroad to cross the state, and it helped to stimulate the tremendous growth of feeder lines, which connected nearly all of Iowa's communities with the national transportation network.

The expansion of railroad routes provided the impetus for Iowa's economic growth, but walking and horses were the modes of travel within and around the towns, and the pace of life was naturally slower with a dependence on horse-drawn vehicles. The sound of clopping hooves, the sight of rows of hitching posts and watering troughs, and the smell of horses were part of the atmosphere. A blacksmith shop and livery stable could be found in any town, large or small. County lines were drawn to allow every resident to drive to the county seat and return home in one day. Travel was limited, and even a short trip was a special occasion. Some farmers made a ritual of going to town at least

once a week, while others went much less frequently. Stores were usually open every night, but shopping was especially heavy on Saturdays, when local farmers and their families would often converge on the nearest village for a break from their regular routine and for a chance to visit with friends.

The first store to be built in a newly settled area was usually a combination general store and post office. The merchant who operated a store performed many business functions for the neighborhood residents. Not only did storekeepers provide goods from wholesale houses in St. Louis, New Orleans, Cincinnati, and Chicago, they were also often involved in any banking or trading conducted in the area. The barter economy present in rural communities required an elaborate system of credit and exchange, and this trade usually centered around the local general store. People relied to some extent on locally produced or handmade goods. A customer would bring in eggs, butter, produce, or perhaps a side of pork or a pelt in exchange for goods at the store. For the rural shopper, only some food items had to be purchased—coffee, salt, and sugar—the rest were grown or made at home. Farmers and townspeople alike depended on a variety of foodstuffs offered by the storekeeper, as well as hardware and tools, utensils, fabrics, and household goods. The growth of banking in Iowa, the increased specialization of shops, and the innovation of mail-order catalogs all helped to change the varied role of the local merchant. However, the tradition of the general store as a town gathering place continued for years.

Some businesses were exclusively the domain of males, including the blacksmith shop, livery stable, and lumberyard, as well as the local saloon. Females dominated other shops, such as the millinery shop and dry-goods store. The commercial stores and specialty shops of Main Street offered a variety of goods and services. Meat markets had raw meat hanging from hooks and sawdust on the floor. The corner drugstore, which often had a soda fountain for social gatherings, offered medical remedies and various personal items. Hardware stores, barbershops, jewelry stores, and furniture and undertaking businesses were also important elements of the town. Individual artisans, like harness makers, tinsmiths, tailors and dressmakers, shoemakers, marble and stone carvers, and carpenters, were among the many skilled workers operating small businesses. The local portrait photographer became an important feature of town life.

Daily and weekly newspapers—the main source of information on national and international affairs, local politics, and gossip—were extremely partisan. Hotels, eating houses, and cafes were the hub of social activities where information was shared and gathered. A sign of permanence for the town came with the establishment of a post office, where townspeople and local farmers came to pick up mail. The coveted position of postmaster came through political appointment. Larger towns had a staff of clerks and letter carriers to deliver mail around town. Rural mail routes, instituted in 1896, expanded to include nearly 300 routes in the state by 1902, spurring the growth of the mail-order business.

Towns attracted professional people such as doctors and dentists, teachers, clergy, and lawyers. With an ability to speak in public, lawyers frequently became the first politicians and were involved from the beginning in land speculation. Merchants and bankers, with their access to capital, were also instrumental in the establishment of new towns. Some landowners and business leaders prospered more than others and used their resources and skills to locate and build towns named in their honor. City founders, if not the rest of the townspeople, believed in prosperity and had an unswerving faith in progress. But as the dwindling number and size of Iowa communities would attest, town developers could not predict how changes in transportation and marketing might challenge the stable economic base of once-thriving towns. Although Iowans suffered during the depressions of 1857, 1873, and 1893, farmers and townspeople alike enjoyed prosperity from 1898 to 1914, a period often termed the Golden Age of Agriculture.

Business and manufacturing concerns grew in part because of their alliance with agriculture, based on the abundance of high-quality products and the needs of Iowa farmers. The meat-packing industry is perhaps the best known of Iowa's early industries. At first, cattle and hogs were driven to a local meat packer, where they were slaughtered and dressed. The meat was salted or smoked so it would not spoil and prepared for shipment. These local packing plants were usually near rivers so that goods could be shipped by boat, but the growth of the railroad feeder lines led to the dispersion of packinghouses across the state. Large processing plants were built in Cedar Rapids, Ottumwa, Waterloo, Sioux City, and other towns. With the development of mechanical ice making in the 1880s, refrigerated railroad cars came into use. Large packers in Chicago and elsewhere cut prices and manipulated railroad rates, forcing smaller packinghouses to close down.

Canning factories and food-processing plants also sprang up across the state, providing nearby markets for farmers' crops and homegrown produce. Seed and nursery businesses, such as Henry Field's or Earl May's, both in Shenandoah, generated a national interest in their goods, largely through their mail-order business. Farm implement manufacturing became important in Iowa and expanded after the turn of the century, when horse power and steam power were gradually replaced by the internal combustion engine. John Froelich of Clayton County is credited with developing the first gasoline-powered tractor, and in 1893 he sold his idea to the Waterloo Gas Traction Engine Company. Later, in 1918, the John Deere Company purchased this firm, thus expanding its already successful farm implement business. The Hart-Parr Company of Charles City and the O. S. Kelly Manufacturing Company of Iowa City also led the way in designing efficient machinery that would simplify and ease the work of farmers.

Industry in the state was not solely dependent upon agriculture for its economic base, and various industries boomed in Iowa for a short time. Foremost among these was coal mining. Countless immigrants from Britain, Ireland, Sweden, Croatia, and other places, along with thousands of African-Americans, worked the mines of Iowa, extracting low-grade bituminous coal, with a high sulphur content.

Stone quarrying was yet another important industry in Iowa and was carried on in several locales in the state. Quarries cut stone for use in building schools, churches, homes, and bridges. They offered a variety of stone: Anamosa, Burlington, Niagaran, St. Louis, and Galena limestone and Sioux quartzite. The limestone bluffs of Iowa also provided lime and cement. The large gypsum deposits near Fort Dodge produced gypsum plaster, wallboard, and other products. The clay and shale deposits allowed for the manufacture of brick and tile at numerous points across the state.

One of the first large-scale industries in the state was lumbering. Because Iowa land was mostly open prairie with little timber, the demand for lumber quickly exceeded local supplies. As a result, huge shipments of white-pine logs from the forests of Wisconsin and Minnesota were rafted down the Mississippi to sawmills along Iowa's eastern border. Preeminent in the lumber trade of the mid- to late-nineteenth century were the names of Musser and Hershey of Muscatine, Weyerhauser of Davenport, Disbrow of Lyons and Clinton, and Farley and Loetscher of Dubuque. The lumber barons of Iowa reaped vast fortunes by converting timber into a wide variety of wholesale and retail lumber products. The milling season lasted from April until November, and when the river was frozen the mill workers were sometimes employed in ice-cutting operations. Companies expanded their lumber trade by creating sash-and-door factories, which produced ornamental woodwork for houses and businesses. Millwork was machine crafted and became inexpensive enough for the average consumer. The popularity of these intricate designs created an enormously successful industry in Iowa. People from all over the country ordered the fancywork for adorning their homes.

Towns across the state supported a variety of specialized light industries. Magazine, book, calendar, and music publishing businesses were operated in some communities. Button factories, glove factories, candy factories, cigar-making operations, an oriental fishery, carriage factories, and breweries are just a few of the business ventures started by these early entrepreneurs and operated by skilled and unskilled laborers of both sexes. Although Iowa has been dominated by its agricultural heritage, the state developed greater industrial diversity after 1900. Many Iowa goods, whether farm products or manufactured items, earned a reputation for quality and dependability.

Labor unions have been active in the state since as early as 1854. Trade unions grew rapidly, with railroad employees forming the biggest unions. There were 1,500 union members in 1885, 45,000 in 1904, and 81,500 in 1919. The years 1919 and 1920 saw enormous labor unrest, which led to a decline in membership at that time. Unions tried to assist working people in time of sickness and unemployment, but among the other issues that the unions worked for were better safety laws, shorter working days, an end to child labor, and old-age pensions.

The industrial development of Iowa coincided with the growth and establishment of economically viable transportation routes. The abundance of agricultural products and the availability of certain natural resources, combined with access to cheap transportation and cheap labor, allowed for profitable investments. The goods produced in Iowa were sold locally or shipped by rail or steamboat to markets in St. Louis, Chicago, or other cities. When the Civil War ended, only 868 miles of rails existed in the state. By 1880, Iowa had 5,200 miles, eventually doubling this to 10,500 miles by 1915. The construction and maintenance of railroad lines, freight and passenger depots, roundhouses, and repair shops demanded an enormous labor force, as did the production and shipment of the coal that fueled the steam-powered locomotives.

The historical forces that shaped the building of Main Street were constantly changing, but the city retained an ordered appearance. Towns were laid out in a rectangular grid pattern divided into lots, with a central village green or courthouse square surrounded by main thoroughfares. The order and regularity of town building reflected the pragmatic and democratic nature of Americans. Though individual expression in building design was part of the tradition, there was a sense of unity and balance in storefronts aligned on a human scale. Common construction techniques—balloon framing or brick walls supporting an interior wooden framework—limited building height to four or five stories until the widespread use of the elevator and structural iron and steel in the twentieth century. False fronts reached skyward, with ornate towers or oriel windows marking corner sites. Signs and advertising symbols identified each storefront and the businesses located on the second floor. Courthouses, public libraries, and department stores were designed on a grander scale, sometimes dwarfing older frame structures.

Main Street was a magnet for the surrounding area, a stopping place and a corridor. Towns were a vital force in community life and helped define a local identity and provide a sense of stability for residents.

The Great Western
Emporium, Ossian,
1860.

And maybe on Saturday night, if the weather was good, you would hitch up the horse and go to town. Some people would go up to eight, ten, twelve miles into town with their horses.

—Oral history interview with Clark Brindle of Conrad, conducted by Roger Raum on March 27, 1977

The W. C. Gannaway General Store, Webb, September 1899. "First store in Webb, then called Glenora." 6 × 8.

[What] were the limits on how far a person could travel, say, to see neighbors or relatives?

Well, if you drove horses, seven miles was about the limit. Of course, sometimes they would go over the limit a little, but you'd have to leave home pretty early if you wanted to spend any time there at all.

That's seven miles one way or round trip?

One way.

Was it common to take trips or go visit for extended periods of time?

No, not very common. We started for Clear Lake one time, and we got up as far as Coulter, and it rained. So that's as far as we ever got. We never got to Clear Lake. We turned around and come back. And it took us almost all day to get back. . . . The going was only about an hour and a half, but the coming back was about four hours in the mud.

—Oral history interview with William Rastetter of Buckeye, conducted by Curtis A. Kennedy on April 10, 1977

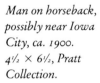

Man on horseback, possibly near Iowa City, ca. 1900. 4½ × 6½, Pratt Collection.

A round grain elevator in Mitchell in the 1870s. The original is a carte de visite owned by George Goeldner.

"Central Blacksmith, Wagon and Repair Shop," Des Moines, 1880s. 4½ × 7½, Lambert Collection.

F. R. Brownell and Company, Sac City, ca. 1900. 5 × 7.

The Crawford and Acheson Grocery in Fairfield. Crawford bought this two-story building in 1862, and after a fire in April 1883 he erected a brick structure as a replacement. 9 × 6½, State Historical Society of Iowa, Des Moines.

The Malvern Milling Company's Electric Flour Mills, featuring roller mills, ca. 1900. Benedict, photographer; 4 × 5, Allen Wortman Collection.

The Sangster Grocery, 210 East College in Iowa City, ca. 1910. 5 × 7, Ebenezer Sangster Collection.

Joe Muto standing by his stall at the City Market in Des Moines, ca. 1919. Original owned by the James Muto family.

The interior of a drugstore in Le Grand, ca. 1908. 6 × 8, George L. Bowen Collection.

C. E. Reeve's butcher shop in Hopkinton. 8 × 10, Mrs. John B. Cox Collection.

A soda fountain in
a drugstore, ca.
1900. 8 × 10.

PRAIRIE CITY

One of the most pleasant men we met was E. B. Tilden, dealer in fancy groceries, canned goods, fruits, nuts, fine cigars, tobacco, etc. Also runs a very fine ice cream parlor; and the only soda fountain in the place. A better place to refresh one's self is hard to find.

—Des Moines *Iowa State Leader*, May 7, 1880, p. 4

May 9, 1878

Take the family to Birmingham to trade and get millinery goods. Not being able to get Eddy a suit in B. he and I go on to Fairfield where we succeed better. Spend a total of $47.49.

—Diary of Alfred T. Giauque of Van Buren County

The exterior of Maring Clothing, showing a window display of men's clothing, Centerville, ca. 1900.

The interior of a dry-goods store, ca. 1895.

The Clement Hardware store in Carlisle in 1910. Harley Clement is in back of the counter, and James Clement is in the aisle. 5 × 8, Clement Collection.

"Hardware store in which M. C. Parsons was a partner," Dubuque Street, Iowa City. 5 × 8.

E. C. Meyer and W. Gibford's barbershop in Newton. Original owned by Rick Hegwood.

A woman's long tresses before it became fashionable to bob one's hair, Malvern. 3 × 4½ glass plate negative, Allen Wortman Collection.

PRAIRIE CITY

Among the recent improvements is a new millinery store lately opened by Miss Dora Keyser, of Des Moines. She occupies a room in a very desirable part of the town, and has it well filled with a large and elegant stock of hats, bonnets, laces, flowers, plumes, and everything to be had in the millinery line. She also carries on dressmaking. Her head workman, Miss Phi. Dohrer, formerly with John M. Knight, of Des Moines, is the lady for the position, and is gaining for her a large trade.
—Des Moines *Iowa State Leader*, May 7, 1880, p. 4

The Casterline Music Store in Tipton, ca. 1900. Frymoyer Collection.

L. E. Burris, Jeweler and Optician, Elliott, ca. 1900. An exterior view is included in chapter 6. 4½ × 12½, State Historical Society of Iowa, Des Moines.

The Bakery and Confectionery next to the United States Express Company office in Sigourney in the 1890s. 6 × 8, State Historical Society of Iowa, Des Moines.

The Bressler Grocery in Des Moines in the 1890s.

The Old Alhambra Bakery and Restaurant, Centerville, ca. 1886. 4 × 4.

A BUSY DAY AT THE City CAFE

The Union Hotel (later the Fleming Hotel), Tipton, 1859. Lane, photographer.

FLEMING HOTEL. TIPTON. 1859. LANE.

Sam Broadus (far right) and friends in a saloon in Charter Oak, ca. 1900. 5 × 7, original owned by Thomas Jones, Jr.

A saloon in Paullina, ca. 1900. 4⅛ × 5⅞.

PRAIRIE CITY

The town until lately had been strictly for prohibition, and not even a billiard table could be found in the place. About three weeks ago King & Dinsmore opened a billiard hall and saloon, but sell nothing but ale, beer and wine, and close promptly at 10 o'clock. They are spoken of as very pleasant young fellows, and are doing a good business.

—Des Moines *Iowa State Leader*, May 7, 1880, p. 4

May 23, 1881
Dentist Ferris of Parkersburg came this forenoon and filled five of my
teeth one for Irving pulled two for Charley 3 for Lena and 3 for Eva
Tooth day.
—Diary of Mary Fisher of Butler County

A man pulling a woman's tooth in the 1860s. From an original one-sixth plate tintype with gold leaf on the instruments and watch chain. William A. Rohlf Collection.

December 26, 1908

Saturday. I was around town part of the day. The "Keep Out" sign for Measles can be seen on many houses here. The Christmas Eve exercises in all of the churches were given up because so many of the children have the Measles.

—Diary of Joshua Williams of Lime Springs

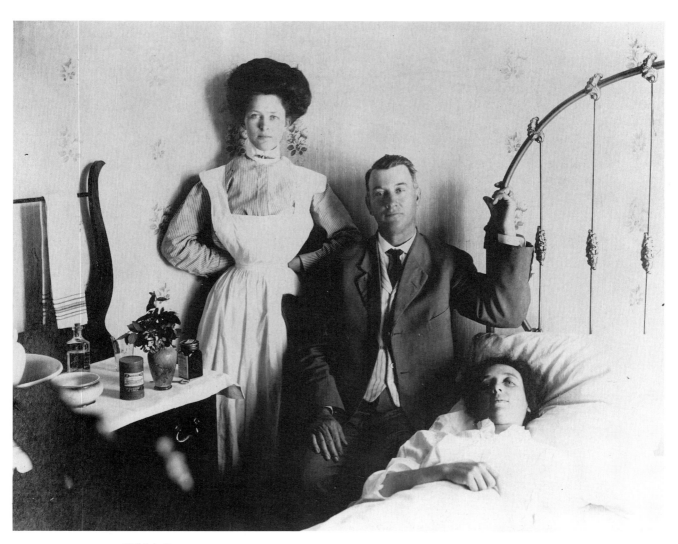

"This is Doctor Tadlock, the nurse and patient. Have been nursing steady since you left here. Have been using three rooms for hospital purposes."
Ca. 1910–1915.
8 × 10.

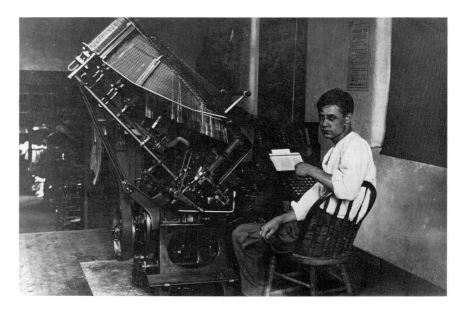

Linotype operator at the Malvern Leader *newspaper office, ca. 1915. 3½ × 5 postcard, Allen Wortman Collection.*

The office staff of Economy Printing, Iowa City, March 10, 1915. William Baldridge, photographer.

Mail sorters, Straw-
berry Point, May
1911. 5 × 7.

Postal carriers in
East Des Moines,
September 1896.
W. H. Nicholas is
on the far right in
the front row.
Northwestern
View Company,
Des Moines, pho-
tographer; 6 × 8,
Prudence Nicholas
Collection.

After ice was harvested from a local river or pond and stored in icehouses, deliverymen brought blocks of ice to customers all over town. Ca. 1900. The fringed nets on the horses allowed them to shake off flies. Cedar Falls Historical Society.

Employees and delivery wagons of the Hawkeye Laundry, Boone, ca. 1905. 5 × 7.

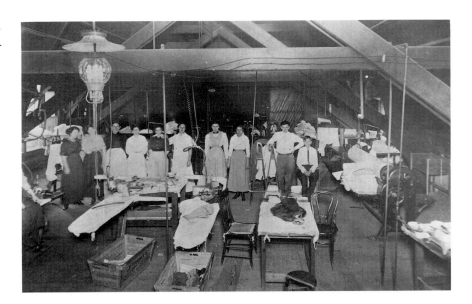

Employees pose inside Taylor's Laundry, Boone, ca. 1910. 5 × 7.

Henry Franke's harness shop in Parkersburg in the 1890s. 4 × 5, Carl Franke Collection.

The Green-Wheeler shoe factory no doubt employs more help than any other enterprise in the city. There are now at work on full time 100 hands with an output of over 400 pairs of shoes daily. At this season of the year, this is remarkable. The five travelling representatives have just started out with their fall and winter samples. With the orders which will be coming in it will be necessary to run the factory at its full capacity through the winter.

—Fort Dodge *Messenger*, September 17, 1897, p. 3

Marble cutting at the Goughnour Brothers monument shop in Allerton. Original owned by Mr. and Mrs. Guy Goughnour.

Axe shop interior, Dubuque, ca. 1910. "Improved woodmen parade axe—designed and manufactured by Buchet & Scheibe." Ernest J. Buchets Collection.

Paint crew in Dysart, ca. 1911–1913. Includes (1) Herman Jessen, (2) William Oehlerts, (3) Louie Oehlerts, (4) John Andresen, and (5) Chris Schmidt. 3½ × 5 postcard, donated by Emma Bahr.

Cigar making in Albia, ca. 1900. C. L. Hyde, photographer; 5 × 8, State Historical Society of Iowa, Des Moines.

Loading fish for shipment, Ruthven, ca. 1912–1917. E. M. Clark, photographer; 3½ × 4¼, E. M. Clark Collection.

Sorting fish at Elgin K. Bruce's Oriental Goldfish Fisheries, Thornburg, 1908. Note the fallen windmill on the hillside. Arganbright, photographer.

*Mending the nets
at Lost Island
Lake, Ruthven, ca.
1912–1917. E. M.
Clark, photogra-
pher; 3 ½ × 4 ¼,
E. M. Clark
Collection.*

*Removing clams
from shells along
the Mississippi
River. 4 × 6,
Florence L. Clark
Collection.*

Let no woman be deterred from any good and profitable employment, for which she is fitted, by the fear of ridicule or opposition. If public sentiment in regard to the work of women is wrong, the quiet, persevering labor of those who have courage to take the lead will soon set it right. Your example is worth more to the next generation than all the income you can command. Educate your daughters as well as your sons; give them a trade or profession by which they can earn a living, and it will be a better inheritance for them than gold or lands. Let the example of your lives be good and the results will be good.

—"The Household," by Nellie Rich, in the Vinton *Eagle*, May 7, 1873

Large rafts of lumber docked at a lumberyard in a Mississippi River town.

The interior of the Farley-Loestcher sash-and-door plant in Dubuque. 8 × 10.

Woodworking in Cedar County, ca. 1910. Frymoyer Collection.

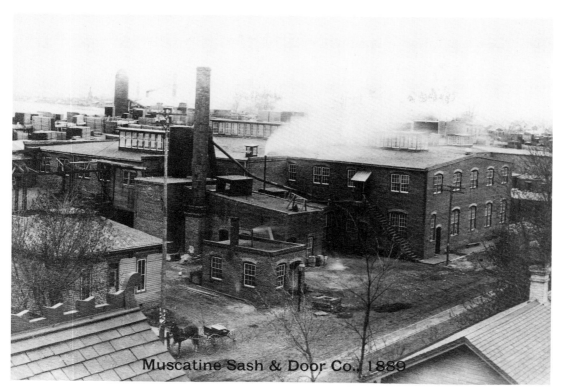

Muscatine Sash & Door Co. 1889

*The Muscatine
Sash and Door
Company in 1889.*

*The interior of a
woodworking shop,
with a fireplace
mantel, West Lib-
erty, ca. 1904.
W. A. Warren, pho-
tographer; 5 × 7
glass plate negative,
W. A. Warren
Collection.*

The Union Stock Yards in Sioux City in 1894. Bornschein, photographer; Sioux City Public Museum.

Immigrant laborers sought employment in the meat-packing plants. This is believed to be the boning room of the Silberhorn Packing Company (later Armour) in Sioux City in the 1880s. Sioux City Public Museum.

SIOUX CITY

"Cudahy-town" will be located east of the packinghouse district, upon one of the most beautiful spots in Morning Side. The house in the town nearest the packinghouses will be three blocks distant from the plant of the Sterling Packing company.

The Cudahy Townsite company has deeds for four blocks in Rustin's addition and has an option on four more blocks adjoining, which will be purchased soon.

Nearly all of this district of eight blocks is on a ridge and the drainage will be perfect. . . . The townsite is near the line of the elevated railway and the residents may make quick trips to the city. Immediate steps will be taken for the improvement of the town. Many cottages will be erected this spring and summer.

No one not an employee of the Cudahy Packing company and a member of the townsite company will be sold any of the lots. There will be a similarity of style in the architecture of the houses, and the town will be one of the attractions of the city. The officers of the townsite company have a high ideal for the settlement, and feel quite sure that in a year or two their streets will be lighted and paved.

—Des Moines *Daily News*, January 12, 1899, p. 3

In drift mining, when the coal has been hauled "to daylight," the small mine wagons are drawn by the mules, or other power, to an elevated platform called a "tipple" and the contents are carefully weighed on platform scales by the "weigh boss." In America everybody is "boss":—"boss-driver," "mine-boss," "fire-boss," "stable-boss," etc.—who is an employee of the operator and is paid monthly. He is assisted in this operation by an individual styled a check-weighman, who is chosen by the miners, and is in their employ, receiving for his compensation a commission of one cent a ton on all the coal mined and weighed over the scales. . . .

The number given to each miner is branded on small pieces of wood or is stamped on small brass checks, like baggage checks. . . . When a wagon is loaded, the miner sticks the numbered bit of wood into an iron staple placed on the side of the wagon, or hangs the brass check onto a hook provided for the purpose. When the wagon reaches the scales the weigh-boss or check-weighman removes the bit of wood or brass, and credits the coal to the number he finds upon it.

—"The Story of American Coals—Part XVI," by William Jasper Nicolls, *Coal Trade Journal* 28 (May 13, 1896): 286

Coal-mining camp, Lehigh, ca. 1910. The large house in the center marked with an O is the boardinghouse. Note the row of miners' homes along the bottom of the hillside. Original owned by Roger Natte.

*Coal mine, 1912.
The coal fields of
Iowa provided jobs
for blacks, Italian
and Welsh immi-
grants, and others
(including children)
who were willing
to work under haz-
ardous conditions.
3½ × 5 postcard,
original owned by
John Jacobs.*

To practically one industry the city of Fort Dodge owes its rapid rise from an insignificant country village to a place of 15,000 inhabitants. . . . To the stucco industry, and practically to that alone must all of this be credited. . . . At the present time about $1,200,000 is invested in the industry that offers employment to some 1,200 men. The rapid growth of the plaster business in Fort Dodge is something of a revelation, and the successful management of the eight large mills now manufacturing plaster of paris, wall and dental plasters by the train load each day has brought millions of dollars to the city.

—Des Moines *Leader*, September 13, 1900, p. 9

Gypsum beds near Fort Dodge, ca. 1900–1905.

The E. J. C. Bealer Quarry, Cedar Valley, with the Cedar River in the background.

Carlton's Perpetual Lime Kiln, Iowa Falls, ca. 1880. From an original stereograph. I. L. Townsend, photographer.

A company known as the Lehigh Clay Works . . . has just been organized at Lehigh. . . . The company intends making all of the common products usually manufactured at a brick yard, including paving brick, building brick, hollow building blocks, tile, sewer pipe and fire brick. It is their intention to inaugurate a department for terra cotta and roofing tile in the near future, but for the present the plant will produce but the more common articles of building material.

—Fort Dodge *Messenger*, March 30, 1900, p. 2

The Sioux City Brick Yards in Riverside, with the Vinegar and Pickling Works at the left, ca. 1894. Sioux City Public Museum.

The Colesburg
Pottery.

*Novelty Iron
Works, Hawkins,
in 1887. The three
men with beards
are the Smith
brothers, the own-
ers of the foundry.
The man marked
with an X is Ellis
Rainard, the boss
and a partner.*
$6 \times 8\frac{1}{4}$.

"When bricklayers wore uniforms." Bricklayers Protective Union No. 5, Sioux City, ca. 1900. Original owned by the union.

CHEROKEE

The Butler-Ryan company, who are constructing the new hospital here, have a full fledged strike on their hands. There are about 200 bricklayers at work on the building, most of whom receive $3 a day. The common laborers or hod carriers and tenders have been paid but $1.25 per day, and it is these who have struck for higher wages. They claim that they cannot live and pay $3.50 a week for board to the Butler-Ryan company who have erected large dining halls and are boarding their help. It averages about two days rain out of the week, which leaves the laborer just $5 for his week's work, or $1.50 to send to his family after paying his board. . . .

The company has advertised in Sioux City papers for common laborers, but so far but few men have been hired, as they will not work for the wages paid.

—Cedar Rapids *Evening Gazette*, June 26, 1897, p. 1

*Illinois Central
railroad workers in
Waterloo. Grout
Museum.*

Workers repairing
track.

*Construction on
the Chicago, Bur-
lington and Quincy
Railroad at Mal-
vern in the 1890s.
Allen Wortman
Collection.*

Le Mars Post: . . . The girls who might have been "hired girls" have sought other avenues of employment and are now found in the shops, stores, offices, school rooms and many other places where men only were formerly employed; and the American families have driven them there. . . . But the "hired girl," the one that families trust the care and keeping of their little ones to, and who often has more brains and better sense than the head of the house, is treated as a slave and the work that she is doing is looked upon as degrading. It will only be a short time when girls for house work can hardly be had at any price.

—Fort Dodge *Messenger*, September 22, 1899, p. 2

A Dysart canning factory in 1916. 3½ × 5 postcard.

The keg washhouse of the Dubuque Brewing and Malting Company, ca. 1895. Klauer Collection, Research Center for Dubuque Area History, Loras College.

The activity at the Heath oat meal mill has been made necessary for the past two months by the large orders being sent out. A force of fifty-one men is being employed and the mill kept running twenty-four hours a day. The output is 700 barrels daily. This is one of the substantial enterprises of the city. The mill is never idle, and the consumption of oats furnishes a ready market for all farmers in this part of the state. The highest market price is always paid for good oats.

—Fort Dodge *Messenger*, September 17, 1897, p. 3

This morning seven colored girls reported for work at the Liddie & Carter overall factory. The factory is in need of help, and when Mrs. Emma Oliphant, colored, applied to C. E. Clark, the foreman, by letter for work for herself and other girls of her race, he replied by letter that they could come, and set this morning as the time for them to begin work. . . . [The seven] called at the factory ready to begin their labors.

Then there was trouble. The white women and girls rose up unanimously and threatened to leave the employment of the company in case the colored girls were allowed to work, and after the discussion had lasted an hour or more, Mr. Clark told the applicants, they say, that under the circumstances he would be compelled to draw the color line.

The girls say that they will report for work again tomorrow morning and until they learn definitely whether they will be allowed to work.

—Cedar Rapids *Evening Gazette*, September 2, 1897, p. 8

CHAPTER 4 : TOWN AND COMMUNITY LIFE

Whether they lived in town or in the surrounding countryside, a centralizing force for Iowans was the hometown or neighborhood. This connection to a town and community provided continuity over time—where a degree of humanity and friendliness permeated relations, evolving into community spirit and civic pride. Togetherness and being neighborly were desirable for residents, as a closely knit community could provide the essential ingredient for prosperity and long-term stability. The dependence on mutual cooperation and informal associations was apparent in everyday business transactions and the sharing of farm work and machinery. Social gatherings offered relief from daily chores and routine business. Though distinctions in social status were clearly known among members of a community, they were seldom expressed or acknowledged publicly. Community members were expected to conform to the dominant code of respectability in order to be regarded as social equals. People would typically speak to one another along the street, and strangers were immediately recognized as such.

The most common form of social activity was daily gossip in which everyone's behavior, especially that of strangers, was closely scrutinized. Judgments about the character and reputation of individuals rested on the extent of their public participation in the community, income and property holdings, mode and style of living, and family background. The negative attributes or misgivings about a person were thoroughly discussed, and yet Iowans were generally considered open-minded folks who could tolerate eccentrics. Still, a maverick could be ostracized from the mainstream of community life. Social conventions seemed so restrictive that some people left in order to explore avenues beyond the limits of small-town expectations.

Formal institutions also exerted influence on the behavior of individuals. Public education was a pivotal force in the development of social skills and training in democratic principles. Educators hoped to instill a sense of responsibility in their pupils, encouraging students to be solid citizens and productive members of society. Even in frontier days, Iowa's residents cherished the value of education, and they sought to establish

Overleaf.
Sleighs lined up around the Monroe County courthouse square in Albia in the 1890s. 6 × 8½, H. Roger Grant Collection.

both private and public schools, schools that were instrumental in the process of Americanizing many foreign-born immigrants.

Although education for the general public was considered desirable, and Iowans have always taken pride in the state's high literacy rate, most people received little more than a fifth-grade education. Before 1920, only a relatively small proportion of the population attended high school, and an even more select group was able to attend a college or university, though some people received training at normal schools, academies, seminaries, and business colleges. A young person was most likely to learn a trade through experience as an apprentice.

The school often became a focal point and a source of pride for the community. In rural areas, the one-room school served nearly every township, while cities built larger schools for several grades. People in the rural school district helped to build and maintain the school building. Teachers were usually poorly paid and sometimes boarded with the parents of schoolchildren. Classes were traditionally in session for two terms, from November (when the harvest was in) until spring planting. Sometimes a short term was offered in the summer. The curriculum stressed the three Rs, but individual teachers often devised their own methods of teaching. With the enactment of a compulsory education law in 1902, which required that all children between the ages of seven and fourteen attend school, Iowa's school system developed further. The improved training and certification of teachers also enhanced the quality of education for Iowans.

At the turn of the century, schools began to concentrate on more practical subjects—those that might relate to the students' future occupations. Teachers taught classes in home economics and manual training in addition to the fundamentals. In rural areas, teachers taught horticulture, livestock care, carpentry, and subjects related to agriculture. The curriculum expanded further with the consolidation of schools, a trend that began with the Buffalo Center–Buffalo Township school in 1899. Consolidation upgraded the quality of education of rural children because more diversified and specialized subjects could be taught in the larger, centralized township schools. Also students could be divided into grades based on age and level of education.

There was resistance to the new concept, and local disputes over district boundaries were common. Many farm families opposed the broader curriculum, which brought urban influences, and the lengthening of the school year seemed a threat to the farming operation, which required the work of the children. Once the idea of publicly financed transportation for schoolchildren was accepted, the consolidation of Iowa's 12,600 one-room schools became inevitable, and the school hack became a familiar sight on Iowa's roads. Coupled with the development of better roads, the real move toward reorganization came from 1919 to 1922, when more than two hundred new districts were formed.

Just as the school and family attempted to indoctrinate young people with a sense of character and morality, religious groups passed on cultural values. The social life of churches dictated codes of behavior for Iowans while also structuring social relations. Among the first to form organizations in the state, church members were involved in social issues ranging from the prohibition of liquor and gambling to swearing in public and dancing. Fellowship and education were important to churchgoers. Religious organizations were among the first to establish colleges in the state.

In a nation characterized by religious pluralism, there were many differing beliefs, so townspeople were able to attend several churches—Methodist, Lutheran, Baptist, Congregationalist, Presbyterian, Unitarian, Roman Catholic, and Quaker, among others. Jewish residents built synagogues. These ties to religion were part of the settlers' and immigrants' heritage and served to form and define societal attitudes and goals. Many churches retained foreign-language services for older members of their ethnic congregations until a World War I proclamation banned such practices. Churches helped to shape upright citizens and contributed to the community by enforcing a strict moral code.

Although the primary function of the church was to provide worship services, members of the congregation also held special events every season—quilting parties, ice cream socials, strawberry festivals, potluck suppers, and temperance meetings. A person's social standing was often determined by his or her commitment to church activities and programs. Of course, there were those who were regarded as heathens for ignoring the code of conduct prescribed by the dominant social class, and every community had individuals who did not follow conventional patterns. Even with great pressure for conformity, most people did not belong to any church or abide by religious customs.

Besides the formal institutions of church and school, Iowans could also seek cultural enlightenment and practical instruction from other sources in the community. Literary societies, music study groups, art circles, lyceums, and debating clubs were popular. Towns were anxious to establish a reputation as a mecca of civilization and culture unparalleled for miles around. As a result, they built opera houses as civic centers for plays given by traveling theatrical groups, concerts and minstrel shows, lectures, and local meetings. Lectures on women's rights, phrenology, and temperance were heavily attended and sometimes brought speakers of national and international fame to many towns across the state. Due to its central location, Iowa became a frequent stopover for celebrities on western tours, from Susan B. Anthony to Oscar Wilde. The level of artistry of some touring groups may not have matched the quality of performance found in larger urban centers, but Iowans demonstrated an enthusiasm for popular entertainment and worked hard to foster local support for the arts.

The Chautauqua movement was at the forefront of attempts to enlighten the public and broaden their intellectual experiences. One of the leading Chautauqua organizations, the Redpath-Vawter Company, originated in Iowa and booked countless musical acts, educational programs, and lectures for performances in towns across the Midwest. The visiting orators discussed the latest scientific discoveries, debated the major political issues of the day, and preached on topics of patriotism and morality. Many of the progressive ideas of the time were expounded on the Chautauqua platform, challenging conventions and leading to a wider acceptance of new ideas when they reached the political arena. The Chautauqua was a major event in a town, involving weeks of planning and participation prior to the event. The introduction of newsreels and feature films in theaters led to the decline of both the Chautauqua and the local opera house. Traditional forms of entertainment for townspeople changed with increased mobility and new forms of communication that directly linked them with the cultural events of the nation and the world.

The formation of fraternal societies and social clubs helped to create a cohesiveness among community members, but at the same time other bonds of local unity were broken by the exclusive character of some groups. Early clubs, especially those started by women, were part of a broader movement toward the expansion of women's roles. While literary and educational societies may have started as small sewing and mending circles, they often evolved into clubs that studied the important issues of the day. Critics charged that the clubs were divisive and had been started by members determined to demonstrate their own superiority. Men's social and fraternal organizations, which were often based on ritualistic meetings and exclusive membership, could divide the community into factions, but these groups did break down barriers based on religious or ethnic differences and fostered a sense of brotherhood and a commitment to community service. Local booster clubs, composed of business leaders interested in promoting the town and civic pride, were especially significant in this respect. The proliferation of clubs ultimately contributed to community solidarity and created common goals for people to achieve, thereby improving the quality of life.

Countless other forces bonded members of a community together. The whole town could not resist involvement with the latest fads and forms of amusement. Baseball, bicycling, roller-skating, croquet, football, and women's basketball were among the most popular sports. Townspeople enthusiastically supported the local baseball team, and games with rival teams served to unify the town and the surrounding countryside in an intense feud with a neighboring community. Entertainment was not limited to sports and athletic events, as musical programs were offered by brass bands, orchestras, and glee clubs. With the passage of the Iowa Band Law, which provided for the collection of local taxes to support a town band, a bandstand located in the center of the town square became a common sight, with weekly concerts by area musicians.

Holidays and celebrations were another seasonal attraction for townspeople and rural residents, with patriotic holidays drawing huge crowds. Local members of the Grand Army of the Republic would lead a procession to the cemetery for a service honoring the war dead on Decoration Day. On the Fourth of July, people hung colorful bunting, waved flags, decorated floats, marched in parades down Main Street, and held dances and contests. Local churches and organizations set up food stands and held bake sales to feed the hungry crowds. On special occasions, local boosters might create a spectacle by sponsoring a balloon ascension or lighting up the evening sky with fireworks. Skillful promoters of a town would plan a special festival, perhaps for the fall harvest, that would attract large numbers of people to the community to do business. Ingenious town leaders, capitalizing on the idea of exhibition palaces that would showcase local products, built large palaces made of corn, coal, flax, apples, bluegrass, and even ice. Townspeople found excitement and thrills along the traditional carnival midway, with its merry-go-round and mechanical rides, and in the tent of a traveling circus, which brought exotic animals, costumed acrobats, sideshows, and clowns. Later, auto racing and flying exhibitions entertained audiences at fairgrounds throughout the state.

As Iowans prospered and more leisure time became available, town and community life evolved. Iowans desired a better cultural life and sought to repeat the patterns of townlife they had left behind when they settled on the frontier. From the beginning, towns laid out central public squares, and later city parks with fountains and immaculate landscaping were designed. They built public libraries, often with the support of town benefactors or with financial backing and architectural plans provided by Andrew Carnegie. Pioneer associations and local collectors built museums to display their artifacts and specimens. The local volunteer fire companies, often combined with police services, grew into professional forces with the purchase of hose wagons and hook and ladder equipment. Towns also improved medical facilities by building modern hospitals. State-run schools, hospitals, and prisons boosted the economy of some towns. Those towns most capable of providing expanded community services, while creating a civilized atmosphere of congeniality and culture, remained the strongest.

Town unity and cooperation were at no time more evident than when disaster struck. Fire could be devastating, destroying an entire business block of frame and brick buildings. Some towns managed to recover and rebuild after such a disaster, but for others a large fire signaled the end of economic growth. The threat of a flood or tornado or a tragic accident such as a train wreck brought together members of the community in excitement and fear. Citizens turned out in droves to survey the damage and offer assistance to the victims.

Some Iowans had immutable feelings of pride and loyalty for their hometowns and with them a sense of obligation to participate in community life. For many, their role as a "good neighbor" was as important as the relationships in their own family. A cohesive sense of community could be achieved only when individuals developed strong personal bonds over a long period of time. These relationships within the community helped people survive the changes between 1860 and 1920. Iowans preserved a rich quality of life, based on values associated with an agrarian tradition and experienced in a small-town setting. While people in urbanized regions of the nation seemed increasingly to lead anonymous lives, characterized by alienation and impersonal relations, Iowans in small towns found continuing security in the predictability of their daily lives.

A class poses in front of a one-room country school.

Always there was hurry to do more than one could possibly do before school at nine a.m. To help with breakfast, put up lunches for five children, eat, wash the dishes and milk cans, sweep the kitchen, harness and hitch up old Ned or the ponies, drive one and a half miles (or walk, sometimes), and put away the team in Uncle William's barn, and get to the schoolhouse by nine o'clock. After school, we changed our clothes, did chores, ironed, or helped with extra jobs to be done, and helped with supper and dishes. Then we had to study, though always too tired to concentrate.

—"School Days," a reminiscence by Edith Mather of Cedar County, ca. 1939, p. 4

Children walking and riding to school, probably in Page County. Samuelson Collection.

The high school class of 1891, possibly in Elkader. The original is a stereograph view, cut in half and bordered with a pink ribbon.

Central High School, "The Castle on the Hill," in Sioux City, ca. 1915. Albertype Company Collection.

School hacks in front of the first consolidated school in Iowa, Buffalo Center, 1896. J. O. Dolen, photographer; 4 × 5.

Schoolchildren with their lunch pails, Palo Alto County, April 15, 1909. E. M. Clark, photographer; 3½ × 5 postcard, E. M. Clark Collection.

Room Two in the Immaculate Conception Academy in Decorah, ca. 1914. 3½ × 5 postcard.

*Arbor Day at the
Thompson school,
ca. 1911–1915.
3 1/2 × 5 postcard.*

Most of the girls preferred to play house under a tree, with broken bits of dishes and perhaps a tiny doll brought from home which could be stowed away in an apron pocket, or else they just preferred to stand around.

—"School Days," by Edith Mather, p. 2

Playing London Bridge and baseball in Page Center, May 2, 1907. 3½ × 5½ postcard, Samuelson Collection.

The Tilford Collegiate Academy in Vinton, ca. 1875. The wagon on the right is possibly the photographer's darkroom. 7 × 9.

A class picture of Jackson Township School No. 5, Sac County, ca. 1907–1908.

*The congregation
in front of the
Methodist church
in Solon in the
1880s. 8 × 10.*

CHRISTIAN CHURCH WOODBINE IA.
E-2679. COPYRIGHTED 1910 BY ST PAUL SOUVENIR CO.

A.P. Cooper, June 19, 1895.
Interior Presbyterian Ch. Wyoming, Iowa.

The interior of
the Presbyterian
church of Wyo-
ming, June 19,
1895. A.F. Cooper
is the pastor. 3 × 3.

The Friday Bible
class at the home of
J.H. Leavitt in
Waterloo, ca.
1910–1915.

St. Mary's Catholic
Church in Nichols,
ca. 1904. W. A.
Warren, photogra-
pher; 5 × 7 glass
plate negative,
W. A. Warren
Collection.

The Grace Meth-
odist Episcopal
Church in Spencer,
ca. 1915. 3½ × 5
postcard.

Quilting in the Lutheran church parlor in North Liberty, ca. 1910. 3½ × 5 postcard, Young Collection.

A Methodist Episcopal Church Sunday School class bobsled party in Wilton in 1906. 5 × 4.

The local rural schools . . . would hold entertainments like pie socials and box socials. The women or the girls . . . would bring a pie, and the young blades, they would buy a pie to get to eat with the girl of their choice. Oftentimes pay a pretty good price for the pie. The proceeds, of course, went to the school. Other types of social entertainments . . . hinge[d] around the churches. There was church parties, ice cream socials, . . . and in the fall months especially . . . they had oyster suppers.

—Oral history interview with Harold Donham of Iowa City, conducted by Alvin Schroeder on March 21, 1977

An ice cream social in Buxton, ca. 1908–1913. State Historical Society of Iowa, Des Moines.

*The Eleventh Iowa
Infantry Band,
1863.*

It would be idle to assert that these celebrations have their origin in pure sentiment. It is usually the business men of the village who see in such an occasion an opportunity for bringing about closer business relations between town and country and, perhaps, of widening the circle of business friends. The matter is discussed in the Commercial Club, a day is chosen and committees are appointed to have the various arrangements in charge. The general place of such a picnic is always the same; a parade in the morning together with the awarding of prizes for various classes of livestock; after dinner a speech, street sports, a ball game and, in the evening, a bowery dance.
—"The Farmer's Picnic," by Hortense Butler Heywood of Peterson,

ca. 1910–1915, p. 2

The Iowa Falls Band in a new bandwagon, ca. 1866–1867. The original is a carte de visite.

A band playing on an Elkader street, August 1884. The original is a stereograph glass plate negative. D. C. Hale, photographer; D. C. Hale Collection.

*A one-man band
entertaining chil-
dren in Chariton in
1896. J. H. Lepper,
photographer;
4 × 5.*

*The Keota Ladies'
Band, ca. 1911–
1912. 3½ × 5
postcard.*

Chase's Mandolin
& Guitar Club of
Muscatine in 1902.
Chase was a music
teacher. Townsend,
photographer;
9 × 13.

March 9, 1905

I was not very well pleased with the show, but no one asked for their money. I discovered last night before leaving the Opera House that the Manager-Palmer [the manager of the show] had stolen some of the tools and props belonging to the house. Home at midnight the Electric lights being cut off, I had to light a coal oil lamp to undress by.

—Diary of Lorin A. Rowe of Eddyville

Lister's Opera House in Newton in the 1890s. Rick Hegwood Collection, original owned by Rick Hegwood.

Two views of the Peavey Grand Opera House in Sioux City, September 24, 1888. Hamilton, photographer; Sioux City Public Museum.

Of late we have been pleased to note the growing interest in study which is manifest among married ladies. This interest seemed to take its first incentive during and near the close of the late civil war and though at first confined to a class, who being made destitute by war were obliged to support themselves, it has so expanded that now it embraces the women of all classes and communities. At the close of the war it was a new feature in school life to see married men and women in the college classes. Now it is a very common thing and we are pleased to note that they are also to be found studying in the normal institutions, in private schools and at their own firesides. Away, and forever, with the idea that a married woman can make no progress in study. It is difficult sometimes to make women believe this and to dispossess them of the idea that marriage is an insuperable barrier to education.

—"The Household," by Nellie Rich, in the Vinton *Eagle*, August 29, 1877

A Chautauqua tent meeting in West Branch, ca. 1910. 3½ × 5 postcard.

A Chautauqua at Columbus Junction in 1913. 3½ × 5 postcard.

My brothers debunked a lot of the things that went on in the midway. They knew that the "Muddy Dora" ate chocolate instead of mud. They knew that the two-headed lady came in with one head in the morning. They learned all that.

—Oral history interview with Mabel Rye of Sioux City, conducted by Leah Hartman on March 16, 1978, p. 8

Children looking at a circus poster, Iowa Falls, ca. 1900. Frank E. Foster, photographer; 4 × 5 glass plate negative, Frank E. Foster Collection.

Taffy pulling on the midway, ca. 1900. Frank E. Foster, photographer; 5 × 4 glass plate negative, Frank E. Foster Collection.

Midway at the fair.

All that a circus represented to some families, that and more the West Liberty Fair meant to us. I can barely remember getting up at 3 a.m. to help in my small way to get the usual work and chores underway. . . .

With our fast team and carriage we usually overtook the plodders before the 9 miles were covered, with bulging market baskets of lunch and dressed in our best—usually stiffly starched white dresses with wide ribbon sashes, the eight of us filed into our carriage. . . .

Two of the children stayed in the carriage while Mother and Father and the rest of us made a tour of the stock barns, the poultry, and exhibit halls of fruits, vegetables, and handcrafts.

Buggies and carriages left without their owners often had lunch baskets, buggy whips, and lap robes stolen, so someone always stayed on guard. The rest of us roamed at will, usually peeking at every stall to judge for ourselves the cattle, sheep, pigs, and horses.

—"The West Liberty Fair," a reminiscence by Edith Mather of Cedar County, ca. 1939, p. 1

The Iowa State Fair and Exposition, Des Moines, August 24– September 1, 1911.

Windmill manufacturers' display at the state fair. State Historical Society of Iowa, Des Moines.

Shortly after six o'clock there is again a rush toward the railway station, on the level field to the south of it stands the huge dark mass of a balloon tremblingly expanding as the gas pours into it. The balloon ascension is the crowning event of the day; as the sun sinks behind the hill and the mist begins to rise from the river, the dark bulk of the balloon rises and expands almost with the effect of a menace.

—"The Farmer's Picnic," by Hortense Butler Heywood, p. 4

A balloon ascension at Riverside Park in Sioux City in 1904. Sioux City Public Museum.

Minstrels or singers performing in Ruthven, ca. 1912–1917. E. M. Clark, photographer; 3½ × 4½, E. M. Clark Collection.

*Members of the
Grand Army of the
Republic in the
Memorial Day pa-
rade, Seventh and
Story streets in
Boone in 1905.*

*Women marching
in a parade, possi-
bly on Armistice
Day in 1919.
3½ × 5 postcard.*

*Children lighting
firecrackers on the
Fourth of July in
Carroll in 1901.
4 × 5.*

*A skating party at
Spirit Lake, ca.
1905. 4½ × 6½.*

Children sledding in Iowa Falls, ca. 1900. Frank E. Foster, photographer; 4 × 5 glass plate negative, Frank E. Foster Collection.

A commencement dance at the State University of Iowa, Iowa City, 1894. P. D. Werts, photographer; 7 × 9.

July 4, 1907

Independence Day. The base-ball game between Cresco and Lime Springs was the chief attraction. . . . We had dinner and supper at the Congregational Church. After supper we saw two balloon ascensions, and the fireworks. . . . Dozens of gallons of ice cream were sold there today, as it was very hot and dusty.

—Diary of Joshua Williams of Lime Springs

A baseball game in Sabula, ca. 1910–1915. Albertype Company Collection.

Long hair, long black hose, full length sleeves, and full bloomers of woolen material for the basketball girls in 1918. Uniforms were a sorry sight at the end of a game; ribbons missing, hair streaming, hose torn, bloomer legs hanging to the ankles because of ripped elastic.

—Elgin Community Heritage Scrapbook

*A basketball game
between Sigourney
and South English,
October 19, 1907.
3½ × 5 postcard.*

A tennis match at Cornell College in Mount Vernon in 1910.

The high jump at the Cornell vs. Iowa State Normal School meet in Cedar Falls in 1903. 4 × 4½.

*A tug-of-war at the
Modern Woodmen
picnic, Ruthven, ca.
1911–1914. E. M.
Clark, photogra-
pher; 3 × 5 photo
postcard, E. M.
Clark Collection.*

Harness racing at Rush Park, "The Lexington of the North," in Independence in October 1890.

They had horse races out there [at the Interstate Fairgrounds in Sioux City], and they were always big events. Dan Patch—you've heard of the most famous race horse of all time?—he ran out there, and all that was real exciting. There was one thing at the races: this carriage would drive into the grounds, and it was all polished up shiny and pretty. It was driven by a black coachman. The ladies in it were all decked out. They had pretty hats, pretty fancy parasols, and everything like that. Well, Sioux City, like all towns still do, they had their house of ill fame—I'll put it like they did then. Now you would call it "the commercial," they were a commercial.

—Oral history interview with Mabel Rye of Sioux City, conducted by Leah Hartman on March 16, 1978, p. 8

The Friday Bowling Club in Davenport in 1907.

The Tabor Gun Club, ca. 1900. 3½ × 5 postcard.

Three men engaged in conversation.

Four men playing dominoes in a store.

No one can successfully maintain a pose under the searching scrutiny of the small town. Nowhere else is one so well known; nowhere else is one so subjected to the acid test for character, and the person who successfully passes the inquiry is a person to be depended upon in all emergencies. . . .

In the really vital things of life, however, we are obliged to forget the prying curiosity and offensive critics. Nowhere else do we find such true sympathies in sorrow, such real interest in our joys, as in the country and country town.

When occasional bits of gossip and speculation come to one's ears, one is first angry, then sincerely amused, and lastly amazed that people can bring such profound interest to such trivial happenings.

Clothes, food, love affairs, disagreements, income, expenditures—no item of one's daily life escapes scrutiny, and when facts are lacking, many of one's neighbors do not hesitate to fall back on surmise and conjecture.

—"Neighbors," by Hortense Butler Heywood of Peterson, ca. 1910–1915

Women drinking beer at Crandall's Point on Spirit Lake in the 1890s. Original owned by Magdalen Hoffman O'Toole.

Motorcyclists in front of a pool hall in Havelock in 1913. 3½ × 5 postcard.

The Old Settlers Picnic in Saunders Grove, Johnson County, ca. 1888.

With dire threats against the weather man if he should be mean enough to prophesy rain for today, a party of about 100 persons, consisting of plumbers and their families, took the steamer W. H. Lehman this morning and went up the river to Mead's Park, where they will picnic today. . . .

During the afternoon field day events will be held with such events as the 50 and 100 yard dashes, potato races, sack races, jumping, etc.

All the plumbers in Des Moines took a lay-off today to attend the affair, some of them driving out to the park in wagons, but most of them going in the steamer.

Two tents were erected on the grounds, from which the refreshments were served.
—Des Moines *Daily News*, July 15, 1897, p. 4

People would go up to Riverside Park on Sundays, and we'd see the streetcars just loaded. They had to take all their picnic things on the streetcar. They would have hammocks, they would have picnic baskets, they would have pillows, they would have everything. How they ever got on I don't know, but they would be just hanging out all over the place.

—Oral history interview with Mabel Rye of Sioux City, conducted by Leah Hartman on March 16, 1978, p. 9

A benefit, "in be-
half of the soldiers
we come," at
the Old Baptist
Church in De Witt
in the 1860s.

Company M of
Montgomery County
leaves Red Oak for
camp in San Fran-
cisco during the
Spanish-American
War, June 1898.
Leonard Schwinn,
photographer; 5 × 8
glass plate negative,
Leonard Schwinn
Collection.

Baggage belonging
to soldiers at the
YMCA at Camp
Dodge in 1918.
4⅞ × 9⅝.

*"On the way
to park for bird
watching,"
Davenport,
ca. 1890.*

*Swimming at
Saunders Park in
Mount Pleasant,
ca. 1915. Alber-
type Company
Collection.*

A Boy Scout troop from Lamoni. The first troop in Lamoni was organized in 1911.

A cooking club in Des Moines. Edinger, photographer.

The Carnegie Library at Emmetsburg, ca. 1914. 3½ × 5 postcard.

An interior view showing specimens displayed by the Sioux City Academy of Science and Letters in the 1890s. 5 × 7.

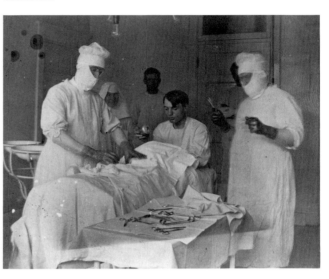

An operating room at St. Joseph Mercy Hospital in Waverly, ca. 1910. Left to right: Drs. William A. Rohlf, L. C. Kern, and O. Chafee. William A. Rohlf Collection.

The Coakley Hospital at Creston, ca. 1910. 3½ × 5 postcard.

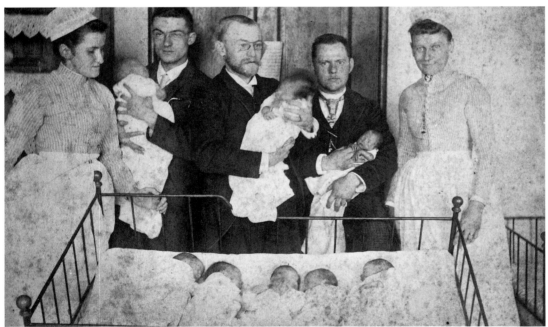

Newborn babies, ca. 1891. Ruml Collection.

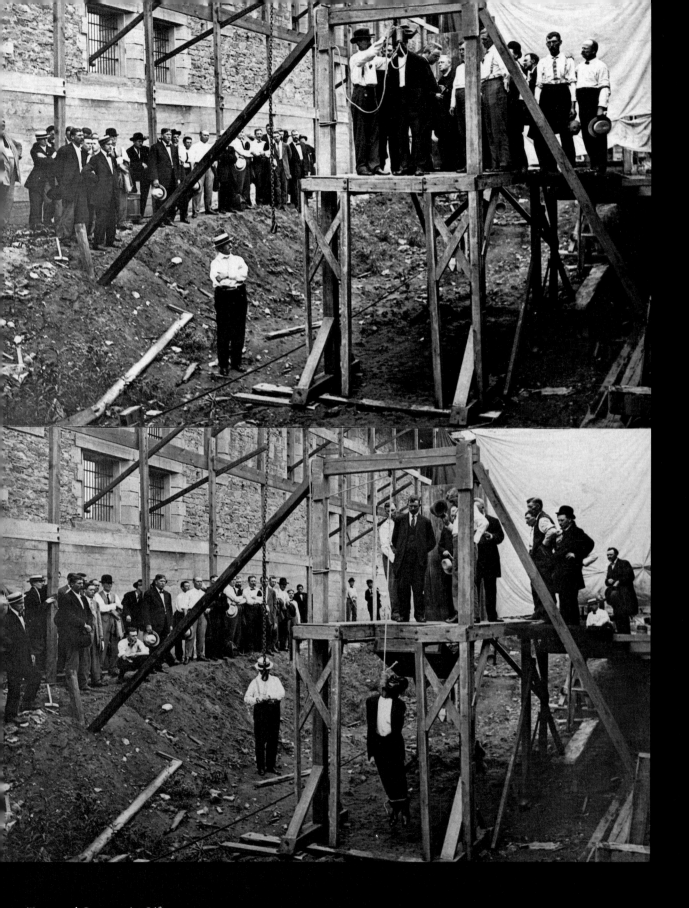

December 31, 1908

J. C. Sanders . . . now warden of the Iowa state penitentiary at Ft. Madison, says that 90% of the prisoners in his charge are there as the direct result of the use of liquor. He thinks it would be a good thing to send some of the bar-tenders, and the men who made the laws licensing saloons, to the penitentiary also.

—Diary of Joshua Williams of Lime Springs

"The Three Grades," three types of prison uniform at Fort Madison, ca. 1915. Jessie White Anderson Collection.

FT. MADISON, PRISON VIEW
THE THREE GRADES.

Two views of a hanging at the Fort Madison penitentiary. State Historical Society of Iowa, Des Moines.

We had the fire tournaments. The fire departments from all over the state would come. They had a skeleton fire station out in center field and we'd go up in the grandstand and watch them practice. Everything was open. You could see the whole thing from the time the signal came and the men jumped up and slid down the pole. The horses leaped out to get under the harnesses, and then they'd race around the track. Whoever did it in the shortest time won the competition.

—Oral history interview with Mabel Rye of Sioux City, conducted by Leah Hartman on March 16, 1978, p. 7

The Rescue Fire Company in the 1890s. 8⅞ × 7½.

The Methodist Episcopal Church fire in Muscatine, Sunday, May 9, 1897. Mary Voy Collection.

The rebuilding of Adair after the fire of 1894. Lloyd Reise Collection.

"Look at this cyclone! We watched it two weeks ago tomorrow from our roof. A regular funnel twister and ho! the damage it did. Iowa is just full of tornadoes this spring. Some more in central Iowa yesterday." Mary Voy Collection.

Above right. *Surveying the tornado damage at the Lobar residence near North Liberty, May 1914. Note the jars of canned goods on the shelves in the cellar. W. D. Crozier, photographer; 3½ × 5 postcard, Jessie White Anderson Collection.*

Floyd River flood damage in Sioux City, May 18, 1892, looking east from Fourth and Court streets. The streets were paved with cedar paving blocks, which, when swollen by the water, exploded and floated away or piled up as in this picture. Sioux City Public Museum.

Surveying a Rock
Island Railroad
wreck near Glad-
brook, March 21,
1910. This wreck—
Iowa's worst rail-
road disaster—took
the lives of fifty-
five passengers and
crew.

Dr. Love and his
family at home in
Iowa City, ca.
1895. 8 × 10.

CHAPTER 5 : HOME AND FAMILY LIFE

Life in town or in the countryside inevitably centered around home and family. Extended families were commonplace in farming communities, and nearly everyone of working age was a part of the family labor force. The surrounding rural area was often inhabited by hordes of relatives—uncles, aunts, and cousins. Family and neighbors enjoyed a social life that included picnics, reunions, weddings, anniversaries, and birthday parties. Families spent their evenings together reading, playing or listening to music, or keeping their hands busy with sewing and knitting. Youngsters entertained themselves by playing dominoes or cards or by looking at a set of stereopticon views. During good weather, families would go on outings in the woods to gather nuts or berries, camp overnight in large canvas tents or in wagons, or go boating and swimming. Hunting and fishing were popular among men, women, and children. Although there was a variety of commercial entertainments and amusements down the street or in nearby towns, many families spent their leisure time in the privacy of their homes, relying on their own imaginations and talents to pass the time.

The life cycle began and ended at home. The structure and activities of a family changed as the years passed, but child rearing remained an integral part of a young family's life. Strict codes of moral conduct and practical skills for survival were taught and incorporated into everyday living. Proper etiquette and manners were expected of middle-class people, and most parents attempted to raise their children as models of themselves. Although formal institutions like church and school shared the responsibility for the children's religious and educational upbringing, the close-knit family exercised the most influence in raising moral, upright young citizens. The dominant domestic cult granted women the primary role in fostering and sustaining family religion, though men were still regarded as the formal head of the household.

The family as a cultural institution passed on traditional values and gender-based roles to each generation. Boys were supposed to learn skills applicable to their future occupations, often assisting with their fathers' work outside the home. They could accompany their fathers to places like the livery stable, where they were exposed to the rudiments of the male world. Girls learned domestic responsibilities such as cooking, housecleaning, and sewing. Middle-class girls were expected to cultivate "feminine" traits and were encouraged to develop talents in music, china painting, or other artistic endeavors. These attributes, along with good homemaking skills, were thought necessary if a woman was to find a good husband and provider, since opportunities for women to attain economic independence were limited. Even as women moved beyond the confines of the home, they still characterized themselves primarily as mothers and nurturers of society. The division of labor within the family placed much of the burden of running a household on women.

No matter what the size of the family or whether they lived on the farm or in town, there was always a daily routine of household chores to be performed. Time-consuming tasks included housecleaning, food preparation, laundry and ironing, and dish washing. Someone had to chop wood and start, stoke, and maintain a coal or wood fire. Many town families had to care for at least one carriage horse, although others rented horses and buggies from the local livery when needed. There were vegetable gardens and flower beds to plant and weed and lawns to tend. Keeping the family's property well maintained and the house freshly painted seemed mandatory for social acceptance for middle-class families.

The centerpiece of middle-class life was the home—a reward for hard labor and a source of family pride and personal identity. The home provided for the domestic comforts and emotional needs of families and served as an expression of the dominant cultural ideal of family togetherness. The tastefully styled home symbolized the decent conduct of private life and the nurturing and love provided by marriage and family life. People arranged their house to fit their daily habits, following the conventional fashions of the time, and made their home a comfortable and affordable setting for relaxation and entertaining. The home itself came to be viewed more as a tranquil retreat from the outside world than as a center of both economic and domestic life, as it had in pre-industrial times.

The increased affluence and an appetite for new styles are reflected in the changing interior views of Iowa homes. A wide selection of manufactured goods was available for purchase in the industrialized society that emerged between 1860 and 1920. Furniture and other household items were mass-produced in designs that mimicked the tastes of the upper classes. Manufactured items were much cheaper than the hand-crafted goods produced by local cabinetmakers and artisans. Beginning in the mid-1880s, the trend in popular literature shifted from promoting Victorian styles of home decoration to emphasizing uncluttered open spaces and classic American styles. The Colonial Revival and the Arts and Crafts movement brought a new aesthetic to middle-class homes, while Victorian styles persisted in some working-class homes and rural areas. To some extent, people were slow to adopt new models of suburban living because they hated to abandon the traditional decorative trappings of taste and status.

Rooms were filled with curio shelves and collections of souvenirs. Popular forms of decoration included framed art prints hanging on walls, potted plants or artificial flowers, seashells, vases, and stuffed pillows with fanciful embroidery work. Photographs appeared propped up on tables and dressers, pinned to curtains, or placed inside velvet-covered albums. Ornamentation and design motifs were often based on symbols from nature—leaves, flowers, fruits, and animals. A typical parlor had densely patterned wallpaper on the walls (and sometimes the ceiling), carpeting or multiple rugs, and curtains on the windows or draping the doorways. If a family could afford it, a piano or parlor organ added to the refined look. The personalized rooms, cluttered with objects, were created to convey a feeling of human warmth and coziness and to express the individuality of the occupants.

Homes were heated with fireplaces, coal-fired furnaces, and wood-burning stoves, which provided a focal point for the family on chilly days. Families set up the parlor stove in the fall and took it down when warm weather returned. The ritualistic spring cleaning of the house sought to remove the coal dust and soot that had settled on the surface of everything. Larger kitchen stoves with range tops and ovens were used for cooking and baking. In working-class homes, people sometimes preferred to socialize in the kitchen, while proponents of middle-class values thought it more civilized to use the parlor for entertaining. Most homes did not have indoor plumbing, so water had to be brought to the house from an outside pump and heated on the stove for dishwashing and bathing. In rural areas, or prior to city water being brought to a house, cisterns collected rainwater for some household uses and for livestock to drink. Outhouses and chamber pots were a necessity despite the inconvenience and unpleasant odor. As families prospered, they updated or remodeled their homes to keep up with innovations and modern amenities, installing bathrooms and kitchen sinks in which water would appear with a turn of the faucet.

The houses of this time could be rustic one-story shelters or two-story frame houses with balloon frame construction. Lighting came from well-placed windows and from kerosene and oil lamps that were handled with great care. Daily rituals and activities were governed by the changing seasons and the amount of available daylight. Gas lighting was available in river towns as early as the 1850s and became even more popular by the 1880s, providing artificial light for nighttime activities. Electricity, also introduced in the 1880s, was often used in combination with gas lighting, but it was not until the turn of the century that it was widely used even in town. As late as 1934, only one-fourth of Iowa's farms had electrical service, and rural electrification did not become widespread in some areas until after World War II.

Living arrangements varied over time, and the houses that Iowans designed and built reflected changes in style, social customs, and the economic status of the owners. The wealthier classes built elaborate mansions that often emulated grand country estates or elegant villas. These homes were richly furnished on the inside and sometimes featured elongated drives, greenhouses, and landscaped gardens. Urban dwellers in Iowa might share housing in a rooming house or rent an apartment or a house. After the turn of the century, increasing numbers of working-class people were buying modest homes.

Iowans, like other midwesterners, chose quite eclectic architectural styles for their homes, ranging from bungalows and cottages to ostentatious mansions. The first structures were basically log cabins or frame buildings, some with stone foundations. Settlers employed simple, utilitarian designs, constructing their homes with available materials and using traditional skills and styles. Later these shelters were replaced by more refined structures, which displayed a variety of architectural styles, including Queen Anne, Italianate, Gothic Revival, and Second Empire.

These newer houses, whether simple frame dwellings or stately homes of brick or stone, testified to the permanence, stability, and success of the builder. Indeed, the owners seemed to compete to demonstrate their prosperity by adding more ornamental woodwork on porch railings and gables and such decorative features as stained and leaded glass. Inside, elaborately carved and scrolled millwork enhanced doorways, staircases, and archways, while outside embellishments included fish-scale or hexagonal shingles and iron roof crestings. Extensions like sleeping porches, terraces, and patios, and devices like window boxes and planters, brought the occupants into closer contact with the natural surroundings.

Although vernacular architecture in Iowa was often a composite of several styles, one common element is featured in stylish homes built in this period. Broad, sweeping porches could be found on many houses, and in good weather this was the favorite gathering place for the family. Porches offered cool breezes and relief from summer heat. Moreover, in small-town Iowa the front veranda was a public gathering place where neighbors would stop by to exchange local news or gossip about almost any topic. Friends and visitors might come to discuss recent marriages or rumors of indiscreet or immoral behavior. People commonly talked about weather and crops, business and politics, or recent births, deaths, and illnesses. The porch helped provide a link between the private side of family life and the broader community.

The home was thus a tangible symbol of a family's standing in the community, proving that the family adhered to the dominant values of hard work, respectability, and decent behavior. The public perception of harmony and tranquility found in an ideal home and family life remained constant even if the private side of life occasionally contradicted this image.

The Ora Barringer
Hymers house un-
der construction
near Ruthven in
1911. George
Chaffee, photogra-
pher; 3½ × 5
postcard.

The Benjamin F.
and Bertha Sham-
baugh home in
winter, 219 North
Clinton, Iowa
City, ca. 1910.
Shambaugh
Collection.

CASEY

During the course of our ramble through the city we noticed some handsome residences. The yards are large and tastefully laid out, the shrubbery beautiful and the flowers fragrant. These people seem to take considerable pride in adorning their homes, and go upon the theory that money thus spent is not thrown away.
—Des Moines *Iowa State Leader*, September 16, 1880, p. 4

The residence of Jasper Thompson in Forest City, 1891. Lancaster and Corey, photographer; 8 × 10, Thompson Family Collection.

When the man threw in the loads of stove-wood, we girls and mother worked like mad while they were gone to cart the wood and pile it in rows against the walls, the chunks in one corner, average size in another, slender sticks in another, and filled bushel baskets with loose bark and kindling. We did this without gloves, and many were the splinters! Before the woodhouse was built, at the same spot there was a wood-pile and we carried wood from the wood-pile to the kitchen wood box. When the wood box was half empty sometimes a toddler was stored here to keep him from getting under foot when there was special haste in getting a meal.

—"Evergreens and Our Family Circle," a reminiscence by Edith Mather
  of Cedar County, p. 26

The F. M. Hicks residence in Monticello in the 1890s. Note the pile of cordwood under the trees at the right. The house was heated with a hot-air wood-burning furnace. Carolyn Hicks, photographer; 4 × 5.

[The icehouse] was filled each winter by three or four sleds and drivers going to the Cedar River at Rochester to cut ice into blocks and haul it the four miles home—a cold and rather dangerous job. In summer this was a delicious place for small bare feet to wriggle into the cool damp sawdust. The refrigerator stood in the west end of the kitchen before the west porch was added. To empty the ice-pan was a responsibility shared in turn as each child grew old enough. But short are children's memories, especially on unusual days, and morning found large pools on the kitchen floor. Mother's irritation was acute that she couldn't be relieved of a *single* responsibility.
—"Evergreens and Our Family Circle," by Edith Mather, pp. 2–3

A miner's home in Brazil in the 1890s. The Ducey family: Charles, John Ducey, Jennifer Buch, Alberta K., Mamie, and Dave Ducey (in front). Original owned by John M. Ducey.

The W. A. Warren
home in winter,
West Liberty, ca.
1904. W. A. War-
ren, photographer;
5 × 7 glass plate
negatives, W. A.
Warren Collection.

The families scattered throughout this area were spoken of as neighbors, and it was not uncommon for a wagon-load of them to drive up on a Sunday morning to spend the day. . . . Sometimes Dolly would have to send one of the girls to the cellar to beat the eggs for the cake, so the visitors would not know she had been caught unprepared.

—"Fragrant Hearts," a reminiscence by Grace Bouler Forgrave about life in Van
    Buren County from the 1840s to the 1860s, original owned by Margaret A. Bonney

Three women posed with a broom, a water basin, and embroidery work in the 1860s. The original is a carte de visite. McDill family photo album.

It was a source of considerable pride when we were big enough to lift the heavy cellar door from the floor to go down cellar. Here there was a dirt floor, and after the furnace was put in about 1890 it was always dusty with wood and ashes. There were boxes and boxes of canned fruit labelled as to kind and year, and barrels of apples which had to be constantly picked over, the most specked ones being made into apple sauce and "Brown Betty."

—"Evergreens and Our Family Circle," by Edith Mather, p. 26

A woman with a mixing bowl in an Iowa City kitchen, ca. 1900. 4 × 5, Pratt Collection.

We had to keep up our room, and we had to do pretty much what our fathers and mothers asked us to do. We washed dishes and we kept our rooms clean and worked in the garden and lawn or whatever, and I don't remember ever questioning our parents' judgment. If we were told to do something, we better do it. . . . Part of our growing up was to obey our parents and be happy about it, and we had a very happy family and I enjoyed growing up very much in a small-town community.

—Oral history interview with Laura Cress of Iowa City, conducted by Denise Flaherty on April 9, 1977

Ellen Mather (left) and family members drying dishes in the kitchen at Evergreens, the Mather farm in Cedar County, ca. 1900. 3 × 4, Mather Family Collection.

Francis Edith Babcock washing dishes, Ruthven, ca. 1910. E. M. Clark, photographer; 5 × 3½ postcard, E. M. Clark Collection, original owned by Glenna Brott.

August 20, 1881

Hannah Scufler the German girl came this afternoon and cannot speak a word of English but seems so willing to work.

—Diary of Mary Fisher of Butler County

*Washday at the
Cooper family
household in
Mechanicsville,
ca. 1900.*

A woman doing laundry on her back porch in Iowa Falls in the 1890s. Frank E. Foster, photographer; 5 × 4 glass plate negative, Frank E. Foster Collection.

Usually the white clothes were boiled in a metal boiler set on the stove where the first suds had been heated and all clothes went through a second cycle. Soap was shaved with a knife from a bar into the heating water. Fels Naphtha, White Laundry, Blue Barrel, or homemade soap from grease and lye—no soap flakes then—was used.

Hard water was "broken" with lye and the resulting scum removed by skimming. Rainwater from a barrel was often used if available and you were fortunate to have gutters on the house to carry rainwater to an underground cistern and a lift pump in the corner of the kitchen.

—"Over My Shoulders," by Wilma Burns, in the *Centennial History Book of Anita* (1975), p. 297

Any woman who can successfully oversee and execute all the varied and complicated work pertaining to general housekeeping, and with the clock-like precision of which many of them are capable, has sufficient brain power to command an army, run a dozen locomotives, superintend the survey of all the wildlands of America, or convert half the heathen on the continent.

—"The Household," by Nellie Rich, in the Vinton *Eagle*, April 2, 1873

A woman, possibly Mrs. Jim Smith, cleaning in Eldora, ca. 1900. Frank E. Foster, photographer; 5 × 4 glass plate negative, Frank E. Foster Collection.

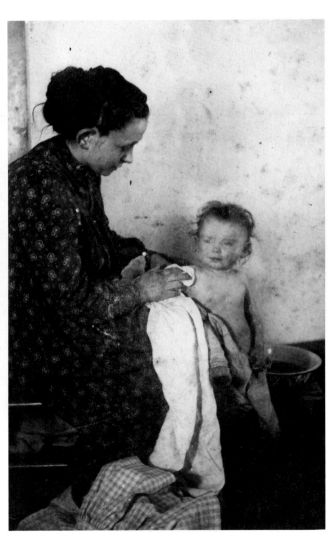

Mrs. J. E. Mather giving her son a bath in Springdale, ca. 1900. J. E. Mather, photographer; 7 × 5, Mather Family Collection.

*Jacob Gabelmann
cutting Ludwig
Gabelmann's hair,
Clarksville, ca.
1920. Karl Walther
or Bertha Gabel-
mann, photogra-
pher; Gabelmann
Collection.*

Gone are the days when every afternoon we sat out in the yard—and friends stopped to visit. Isn't this serene? And grandma would soon come out with the hired girl carrying a pitcher of lemonade. The way I remember it, it was an everyday affair— no one was busy except papa and he'd soon be driving up, tieing the horses to the hitching post and joining us.

—Reverse side of the photograph of the Haugen family

The Gilbert Haugen family on their lawn in Northwood, ca. 1905. 4½ × 6⅝, Haugen Collection.

The lard lamps then used were by no means equal to our electric lights. Later they made their own candles, which were used very sparingly, one for ordinary occasions, two if the children wished to study, and three when Great-grandmother sewed on black.

—"The Story of My Grandmother," by Helen Augusta Larrabee, an entry in the State Historical Society of Iowa's essay contest, 1923

A family spends an evening together in Ames in the 1880s. Note the bowler hat at top of photo, probably used to mask the glare from an overhead light. The original is a stereograph view owned by George Goeldner.

It was the family custom to gather around the fire on winter evenings. James would crack nuts and roast apples. One of the girls would read aloud while the others would knit or sew, "resting work," they called it.

Remembering the yards of stitching and knitting, all the garments that were fashioned by hand, we could understand Susan's impatience with those who were content to sit with "idle hands."

—"Fragrant Hearts," by Grace Bouler Forgrave

The Neal family in Keota, ca. 1895. "This picture is the photographer's self portrait with family." The boy is looking through a stereopticon viewer.

The back parlor was the last word for a gracious home of that period. Here were found the glory of the household furniture—the handsome walnut bookcase with glass doors bought with mother's school-teaching money and Uncle Eddie's oil portrait. Here was the walnut stuffed "parlor set" which consisted of a love seat, a Turkish rocker, and four of the six straight chairs. The other two, and the big armchair, were in the parlor. A walnut center table stood under the white-shaded hanging lamp. . . . A pair of Nottingham lace curtains hung from a gilt lambrekin over the west window.

—"Evergreens and Our Family Circle," by Edith Mather, p. 23

I suppose the telephone and the sleeping porch were put in about 1900. The automobile appeared about 1912, and the radio about 1925. Rachel gave the Victrola to Mother about 1917. The bathroom and upstairs to the kitchen were put in the summer of 1902.

—"Evergreens and Our Family Circle," by Edith Mather, p. 23

People sitting around a dining room table in the Schwinn home at 707 Reed in Red Oak, ca. 1896–1905. Note Leonard Schwinn and his camera reflected in the mirror on the sideboard.

6½ × 8½ glass plate negative, Leonard Schwinn Collection.

The McFarland family gathered around their dining room table in Clinton, ca. 1916. 3½ × 5 postcard, McFarland Family Collection.

The interior of the Vigars family home in rural Moville, ca. 1911–1914. The man on the far right is R. J. Vigars, the photographer. He is probably using a long cable to trip the shutter release on the camera. R. J. Vigars photo album.

A bedroom, ca.
1900. 3½ × 4½,
Pratt Collection.

The nursery or
girls' room on the
second floor of
Montauk, the
home of William
Larrabee and
his family in
Clermont, ca.
1899. Larrabee
Collection.

The old method of hair curling, ca. 1900. Note the curling iron in the chimney of the kerosene lamp on the dresser. Frank E. Foster, photographer; 5 × 4 glass plate negative, Frank E. Foster Collection.

A man in sleep-wear, Iowa Falls, ca. 1900. Frank E. Foster, photographer; 5 × 4 glass plate negative, Frank E. Foster Collection.

The sitting room.

The parlor. Note the corner of the stove.

The parlor.

We had a very large house. It was a typical house that was built in that era, where you have a kitchen, living room, dining room, and then what they called the parlor. Now, our piano was in the parlor, and the parlor was just kept for—well, you never used it. It was just an extra room. I think they used it if they would have funerals, or if you had somebody special coming, you might use the parlor.

—Oral history interview with Mrs. Fred Schlott of Council Bluffs, conducted by
James Schlott on March 21, 1977

The parlor.

An interior view of
the Benjamin and
Bertha Shambaugh
home at 219 N.
Clinton in Iowa
City, looking to-
ward the library
and the dining
room from the
front room, No-
vember 1904.

Coover, photogra-
pher; 7⅞ × 9⅞
glass plate nega-
tive, Shambaugh
Collection.

The interior of the Shambaugh home, looking into the front room from the entrance hall. Coover, photographer; 7⅞ × 9⅞ glass plate negative, Shambaugh Collection.

The interior of the Shambaugh home, looking into the dining room from the library, November 1904. Coover, photographer; 7⅞ × 9⅞ glass plate negative, Shambaugh Collection.

A back room on the first floor of Montauk, the home of William Larrabee and his family in Clermont, 10:05 A.M., February 3, 1899. Larrabee Collection.

A sitting room or parlor on the first floor of Montauk, ca. 1899. Note the wicker furniture, which was immensely popular at this time, and the profusion of geraniums on the windowsills. Larrabee Collection.

Playing cards in the "shop" at Montauk in the 1890s. Left to right: William Larrabee, Jr., Frederic Larrabee, Charles Larrabee, and brother-in-law Don Love. Larrabee Collection.

A card game behind the barn, rural Kensett, ca. 1900–1910. 4 × 5 glass plate negative, Nels L. Roslien Collection.

For the young people . . . we had house parties. We rolled the rug up, the home . . . had a Victrola and records, we danced to records. There was always someone, of course, that played an instrument—a guitar, a banjo, mouth organ—and many times we furnished our own music.

—Oral history interview with Harold Donham of Iowa City, conducted by Alvin Schroeder on March 21, 1977

Nels L. Roslien with an Edison gramophone, rural Kensett, ca. 1900–1910. 5 × 4 glass plate negative, Nels L. Roslien Collection.

H. Claude Horack
(left) and Frank E.
Horack with a
string of gamebirds
in the backyard of
the Horack home
in Iowa City, ca.
1893. Bertha M.H.
Shambaugh, pho-
tographer; 4⅞ ×
7⅞ glass plate nega-
tive, Shambaugh
Collection.

Frank E. Horack
and his taxidermy
specimens in Iowa
City, ca. 1893. Ber-
tha M.H. Sham-
baugh, photogra-
pher; 4¾ × 7⅝

glass plate nega-
tive, Shambaugh
Collection.

Herbert Smith playing golf, with Mary Sanders as his caddy, in Iowa City in the 1890s. 6¼ × 4, Sanders family photo album.

The Kelly family playing croquet in Red Oak, ca. 1895–1905. Leonard Schwinn, photographer; 5 × 7 glass plate negative, Leonard Schwinn Collection.

A picnic at Mc-Gregor in the 1880s, with a fresh catch of fish. State Historical Society of Iowa, Des Moines.

A picnic, ca. 1904. W. A. Warren, photographer; 5 × 7, W. A. Warren Collection.

The Mather family camping along the Cedar River in Cedar County in 1900 or 1901. J. E. Mather, photographer; 5 × 7 glass plate negative, Mather Family Collection.

A woman (Anna Larrabee?) in a rowboat, near Clermont in the 1890s. Note the guitar in the left foreground. Larrabee Collection.

The Mather family
boating, probably
on the Cedar
River, ca. 1900.
J. E. Mather, pho-
tographer; 5 × 7
glass plate negative,
Mather Family
Collection.

July 2, 1881

The Lady hair dresser combed my hair and then I sat for some photographs. In the afternoon we all went to Clear Lake took the Lady Franklin Steam Boat and crossed the Lake. Roamed about on the beach ate our luncheon and at sunset crossed the Lake and drove home.

—Diary of Mary Fisher of Butler County

The steamer Oko-boji on Lake Oko-boji, ca. 1900. Note "Stowes Superb Band" on the upper deck. 4 × 5.

The shores of the creek changed in contour with big rains and we'd find some favorite peninsula gone for good. We played fishing, building dams of stones and branches, also bridges. Excitement was high when we discovered a mud-turtle. Didn't we try to make him bite and hang on to our sticks so we would drag him to the house? Turtle meat was a delicacy.

—"Evergreens and Our Family Circle," by Edith Mather, p. 11

Children fishing off a dock on Clear Lake. Note the toy sailboat in the water. 4 × 5.

Arthur Allen and his dog near Lost Island Lake, Ruthven, ca. 1912–1917. E. M. Clark, photographer; 5½ × 3½ postcard, E. M. Clark Collection.

*Children with a
dog hitched to a
cart, possibly near
Williamsburg. The
original is privately
owned.*

*Wilma (left) and
Hazel Warren
playing with a doll
and corncobs, West
Liberty, ca. 1904.
W. A. Warren, pho-
tographer; 5 × 7
glass plate negative,
W. A. Warren
Collection.*

*A boy on stilts,
Bentonsport, ca.
1903. From an
original glass plate
negative owned by
Oneita Fisher.
Effie Seward,
photographer.*

"He investigates a fortune telling tent," one of a series of photos of children playing, Ruthven, August 3, 1910. E. M. Clark, photographer; 3½ × 5 postcard, E. M. Clark Collection.

Henry Platner about to take a swing with his baseball bat, Mount Vernon, ca. 1905. 5 × 3½ postcard, Moffit Collection.

William E. Platner and his family, Mount Vernon, ca. 1905. Henry Platner is the boy at left. 3½ × 5 postcard, Moffit Collection.

A girl with presents
under a Christmas
tree, Dubuque, ca.
1910–1920. 5 × 7
glass plate negative,
Ernest J. Buchets
Collection.

The wedding of Oscar O. Salomonson and Jorgina I. Rosheim, Scarville, October 7, 1907.

A coffin with flowers. State Historical Society of Iowa, Des Moines.

Oliver Stephen-
son and his family
outside their
home three and a
half miles west
of Swedesburg,
ca. 1889. Hel-
ene Thomson
Collection.

A Buxton family in front of their home, ca. 1905–1910. State Historical Society of Iowa, Des Moines.

The McNabb family home in Delta, ca. 1910. Shown are Missouri Myers McNabb and her husband, Phillip, and their daughter, Pearl. Their horse was named Pet and their dog, Nellie. 6¼ × 8¼.

CHAPTER 6 : COMING OF AGE

The history of Iowa from 1860 to 1920 followed a pattern similar to that of other midwestern agricultural states. Although the state's history can be seen in the context of the national experience, the development of Iowa does not directly parallel the growth of the nation as a whole. While some parts of the nation came to be dominated by one or more industrial cities, Iowa remained agricultural, rural, and characterized by small towns. The shape and direction of life in Iowa continued to center around the traditional values associated with country living.

Rural America has been regarded as the cradle of democracy, the stronghold of rugged individualism tempered by a moral ideology. The Jeffersonian and Jacksonian ideas, espoused during the frontier era when Iowa was settled, emphasized a close association with the land and a belief in democratic ideals. This philosophy was well suited to the Iowa experience. Independence, honesty, and moral integrity were the publicly articulated qualities sought in individuals. These attitudes sprang directly from the cultural past of those who migrated to the state—Yankee settlers from New England, pioneer families from the Ohio River valley, and a constant influx of foreign immigrants.

Those who came to Iowa were seeking freedom or a change in their prospects. They hoped for a chance to improve their economic situation by obtaining new land in a region full of promise. New arrivals rode in covered wagons, walked, and traveled by steamboat until railroad lines expanded frontier horizons. Iowans wanted to establish a stable society with permanent political, economic, and cultural institutions—a society patterned after their past experiences in other parts of the country or in foreign lands. They hoped to fulfill the American dream of creating a better life, forming a state in the heart of the nation with distinctive cultural values that survived over several generations.

Iowans were sometimes suspicious of recent immigrants, who brought differing religious beliefs, strange languages, and patterns of living that natives were unaccustomed to. The immigrants were perceived as a threat to traditional American values. Although Iowans publicly professed a high degree of tolerance, racial and ethnic prejudice did exist. The exclusion of certain segments of society from involvement in public affairs

The transition from the horse and buggy to motor vehicles could not be complete until highways were paved and rural roads were improved with gravel.

was common, and those in power could deny or limit opportunities. In essence, this was a patriarchal society, governed by middle- and upper-class white males whose traditions and values came from England and northern Europe. Though confined by this system, women made significant (though often unrecognized) contributions outside of their customary roles as wives and mothers, shaping the character and identity of their communities. There were no dramatic shifts in this cultural identity until after 1920. At that time, federal laws restricting immigration were passed and women obtained the right to vote.

The twentieth century ushered in tremendous economic, political, and social changes that radically altered the lives of most Iowans. Earlier, there had been a close relationship between town and countryside, but gradually their economic interests diverged and tensions and hostilities arose. The virtues of farming and the values associated with nineteenth-century agrarian philosophy were being challenged and replaced by new morals and customs spawned by urban growth and rapid technological innovation. Rural America was increasingly portrayed as isolated and plagued by restricted opportunities, while the city offered bright lights and modern conveniences. The conflict intensified as the rural dwellers grew ever more suspicious of the city, which they viewed as evil, indecent, and corrupt. More than that, those in the countryside feared that the attractions of the city would draw young people away.

Still, the city held promise and a cosmopolitan atmosphere not found in a simple rural life. Once the economic base for an urban area had been firmly established, the residents expanded on their earlier notions of progress. As towns matured and cities grew, municipal services and civic pride flourished. Citizens came to expect more public services to provide the conveniences and refinements found in larger communities. Water plants, reservoirs, and water towers were built by private companies and municipal governments, and in the 1880s some towns laid out sewage disposal systems. The sprinkler cart sprayed dusty streets regularly, and rubbish baskets were set up on corners. Dirt streets were paved with bricks and cedar blocks, and later cement and asphalt paving arrived. Wooden sidewalks and walkways at intersections helped keep people's feet dry. These, too, were eventually replaced by concrete sidewalks and curbs. Improved street lighting was set up to illuminate residential avenues and business districts.

The growth of public utilities and electric power plants also changed urban life. A large hydroelectric dam and shipping lock were built on the Mississippi River at Keokuk in 1913, generating power for southeastern Iowa. Smaller hydroelectric dams served towns along Iowa's interior rivers, while steam engines generated power at other plants. The power lines erected by utility companies did not extend very far into the countryside, however, ultimately creating a cultural lag between town and rural dwellers and hindering the latter's ability to adopt new labor-saving devices.

Railroads provided an important link between towns, and the depot served as the gateway to the city. With 10,493 miles of railroad track in 1915, Iowa ranked fourth in the nation. Trolley and interurban lines provided transportation to the larger business districts from outlying areas. Railroads and commuter trolley lines gave rural and small-town dwellers the opportunity to shop and work in large metropolitan centers. Iowans were part of an increasingly mobile society, with perceptions of the limits set by time and distance permanently altered.

In a similar fashion, the development of improved communication systems put Iowans in touch with the rest of the world, helping to counter rural isolation. Although the first telephones were in use by the early 1880s, the primary growth of independent companies and systems came between 1890 and 1917. By 1917, 86 percent of the rural households in Iowa had at least one telephone. The independent companies that created local party lines in the farm neighborhoods did not immediately hook up with other rural lines or town systems, but eventually lines were consolidated and linked. An extensive network of telephone and telegraph lines allowed for immediate nationwide communications, which improved news-gathering techniques and spawned a new era of advertising.

Mass advertising promoted the use of ready-made goods and encouraged a drift toward national conformity. National and regional magazines discussed the popular issues of the day and brought new information and images into the homes of Iowans. Mail-order catalogs advertised a wide assortment of manufactured goods, ranging from household furnishings and tools to cameras and even automobiles. Rural free delivery spread rapidly after 1896, and the introduction of parcel post in 1913 allowed people to purchase items from all over the country. Though railway express companies had shipped consumer items for many years, rural free delivery brought items right to the farmer's front door, an idea that many small-town merchants found to be a threat to the local economy. The distinct rural culture gave way as mass production and distribution raised the standard of living in the country and made farm life more like town life. In earlier years, people had enjoyed a degree of independence from the outside world and could function within a limited sphere, but interaction with a more diverse national scene was inevitable.

Iowans were exposed to a mainstream national culture whose new inventions and consumer items created subtle and profound changes in their lives. Improved washing machines and electric irons eased household drudgery. Gramophones brought recorded music into people's homes. In 1919 the first radio broadcast was transmitted to Iowans.

Motion pictures and newsreels also contributed to the modernization of an older, more traditional society. Improved literacy, increased travel, and new forms of communication all brought cultural enlightenment to Iowans. These outside influences—whether technological, economic, or political—challenged and expanded people's knowledge and changed their perceptions of the entire world.

Some aspects of modern life caused people to question traditional values and social conventions. The revolution in transportation brought on by the invention of the gasoline engine is one example. In 1906 there were only 1,000 automobiles in Iowa, and they were usually owned by bankers, town merchants, and country doctors. Autos were still considered unreliable and expensive, and road conditions were poor. The development of the Model T changed attitudes among country folk, and by 1910 farmers were buying half of all the autos sold. By World War I the automobile was becoming a necessity for town and farm families. Local blacksmiths converted their shops into auto garages, and soon people were campaigning to have nearby roads and highways paved. With 171,575 automobiles on Iowa farms by 1920, the auto and truck were helping to increase mobility in rural areas, lessen isolation, and provide a new method of transporting products to market. The Good Roads Movement, supported by Iowa farmers and business leaders, and the new state highway commission drastically altered the Iowa landscape over succeeding decades. Highways and farm-to-market roads provided access to areas not reached by railroad routes. The transition from horse-and-buggy days to the faster-paced days of the automobile took many years, but by 1920 life in Iowa had already been changed in a dramatic and irreversible way.

At the same time, farmers wanted to take advantage of modernization and improve their standard of living. The result was the transformation of the family farm into a business operation. Farmers realized they could obtain greater profits if they practiced more efficient farming methods. Various people—including college professors, county extension agents, newspaper and magazine editors, and politicians—stressed the need for improved, scientific farming. During World War I, campaigns declaring "Food Will Win the War" encouraged farmers to begin implementing the ideas of the "new agriculture" in order to increase production. After the war, the loss of export markets and the collapse of falsely inflated land values led to a severe agricultural depression beginning in 1920, as farm income dropped by 50 percent. Improved methods did not insure better prices, because farmers were overproducing for the peacetime market. Their inability to make loan payments or to pay taxes often led to bankruptcy and the loss of the family farm.

In 1860 there were 675,000 people living in Iowa, a figure that rose to 1.2 million by

1870 and 2.4 million by 1920. The population of Iowa then remained relatively constant until after World War II. The shift from rural to urban living continued, albeit at a slow pace. By 1956, those who lived on farms or in towns of less than 2,500 made up half of the population, while the other half lived in about 100 urban centers.

Iowa is a collection of small towns of varying size, with the vast majority containing fewer than 500 people and many fewer than 100. There are about fifty small cities of over 5,000 people and only about fifteen regional centers of over 10,000. Des Moines was the only town destined to become a large metropolitan center, although six cities—Sioux City, Waterloo, Council Bluffs, Cedar Rapids, Dubuque, and the Davenport area—could be classified as major urban areas. Many towns that were once thriving and prosperous have vanished from the landscape. More than 2,200 villages and hamlets were abandoned between 1840 and 1930. The number of family farms continued to diminish even as the average size increased. Many farmsteads were as small as 80 acres, though the average size of a farm in Iowa reached 155 acres by 1935. With 94 percent of the state presently classified as farmland, Iowans still find continuity in their agricultural heritage.

Iowa matured in an era steeped in agrarian values, and the character of Iowa reflects this agricultural and rural background. Despite all the changes, most Iowans have somehow managed to cling to traditional beliefs and attitudes even though twentieth-century living has blended urban and rural values. Iowa was involved in a process of constant change, but different parts of it changed at different rates. Small-town beliefs changed more slowly, giving longer life to an older generation's reassuring platitudes and timeless certainties. Nonetheless, Iowa mirrored the nation as a whole and responded to changing conditions, new perspectives, and new principles. As American society became essentially urban, a transformation took place in the agricultural hinterland spawned by technological and managerial revolutions in nearly every arena.

Iowa's rural communities and small towns were coming of age by 1920. The older generation watched their children choose careers and roles that differed from their own, while young people rejected some of the outmoded ideas from the past. Still, the state's rural heritage of strong kinship networks, of neighbor helping neighbor, and of a solid work ethic prevailed, providing stability and continuity. Part of this enduring cultural identity has been documented and thus preserved in the visual record of Iowa's past. The imprint left by those who lived during this period helps us understand their rich legacy.

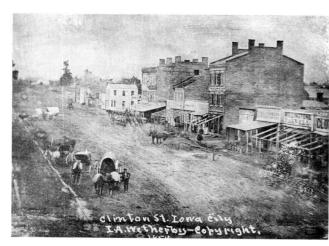

Clinton Street storefronts in Iowa City, 1854 or 1856. From an original daguerreotype. Isaac A. Wetherby, photographer; Isaac A. Wetherby Collection.

A Clermont street scene, in the 1870s. The image is reversed because the original is a tintype. 5 × 4, Larrabee Collection.

*The first streetcar at
Eighth and Main in
Dubuque in the
1870s. The original
is a stereograph
view.*

"New Americans," passengers from the steerage section of a steamer heading across the Atlantic. These immigrants were photographed by a member of the William Larrabee family returning from a trip abroad, ca. 1901. Larrabee Collection.

The steamboat Colorado, probably on the Missouri River. H. L. Broadbelt Collection.

A Diamond Jo Line steamboat with a four-barge tow on the Mississippi in 1875. Original owned by William J. Petersen.

Des Moines is pre-eminently the railroad center of Iowa. . . . The roads radiate from the city like the spokes of a wheel, and bring into direct connection with Des Moines the entire territory of the state of Iowa, gridironed as it is with railroads, and of which it is said that there is but one point in the state that is fourteen miles from a railroad line. . . .

There are thirteen spokes in this wheel, whose hub is at Des Moines: thirteen railway lines radiate from the city. They are controlled by seven systems as follows: Chicago and Northwestern, Chicago Great Western, Chicago, Rock Island & Pacific, Wabash, Chicago, Burlington & Quincy, Des Moines, Northern & Western, Chicago, Milwaukee & St. Paul, Minneapolis & St. Louis, and the Des Moines Union railway company, which controls terminals in the city and lines of entrance to the town. . . .

On the lines of road enumerated there are eighty-four passenger trains in and out of the city every twenty-four hours, besides scores of freights. These trains give the city connection with the great commercial centers in every direction. Chicago and the east, St. Louis and the south, Council Bluffs, Omaha and the west, St. Paul, Minneapolis and the north and northwest, Kansas City and the southwest, and all reached by direct trains from Des Moines.

—Des Moines *Leader*, January 5, 1896, p. 18

*The Union Depot
in Burlington
served passengers
on the Rock Island
and the Chicago,
Burlington and
Quincy Railroad
lines. Built in
1882, this building
burned on January
20, 1943.*

A conductor handing out reading matter to passengers on the Chicago, Burlington and Quincy Railroad, ca. 1900.

A crowd near the railroad tracks in Decorah, ca. 1900–1905. Reynolds, photographer.

February 16, 1905
This forenoon I was called by my son in Ottumwa over the phone saying that his babe had died the night before. Wray Torrey and I went down on the 10:00 o'clock train.

—Diary of Lorin A. Rowe of Eddyville

A view of the Central City depot taken from the top of a railroad boxcar in 1910.

A ferry that oper-ated between Du-buque, Iowa, and East Dubuque, Illi- *nois, ca. 1880. The original is a stereo-graph. Melendy-Rider Collection.*

The first bridge across the Cedar River at Waterloo, in the 1870s. The bridge was erected in 1859. This view looks northeast from below the *west end of the bridge. 5¼ × 7¼ oval.*

Warren F. Musser with his hack in Mason City, in the early 1870s. Musser worked for the Milwaukee Railroad.

An electric trolley car run by the Cedar Rapids and Marion City Railway Company, at the Kenwood Park station, 1898. Note the passengers visible through the windows.

The Third and Jones station of the elevated railway in Sioux City. Waltermire, photographer; Sioux City Public Museum.

"First photo taken of Decorah, Iowa," ca. 1867–1870. H. P. Field Collection.

Main Street looking south in Paullina in the 1890s. "Paullina Hotel at the extreme right in foreground. Presbyterian Church in the background. The white frame public school [is] to the right of the church."

*A bird's-eye view
of Fenton.*

A bird's-eye view of Lansing, ca. 1900. Note the stacks of lumber.

West side of Main
Street, Malvern, ca.
1904. Note the blur
caused by the mov-
ing automobile at
the far right.
Allen Wortman
Collection.

"A dull Saturday"
in Akron in August
1894. Fred H.
Patch of Sioux
City, photographer;
8 × 10.

*Portion of a pan-
oramic view of
Boone, ca. 1907.
Frederick J. Band-
holtz, photogra-
pher; Library of
Congress.*

*Street scenes in
Elliott, ca. 1900.
4 × 12½, State
Historical Society
of Iowa, Des
Moines.*

A view of Oelwein, ca. 1907. Frederick J. Bandholtz, photographer; Library of Congress.

A view of Iowa Falls, ca. 1907. Frederick J. Bandholtz, photographer; Library of Congress.

Portion of a panoramic view of Sheldon, ca. 1907. Frederick J. Bandholtz, photographer; Library of Congress.

A portion of a panoramic view of Waterloo, ca. 1911–1914. Note the various modes of transportation—the autos, wagons, buggy, goat cart, and trolley. Haines Brothers, photographer.

*The Humboldt
Electric Light and
Power Company
plant, built in 1898.*

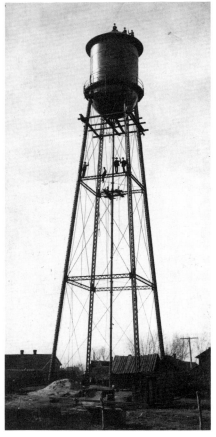

*Building the water
tower at Sumner,
ca. 1903–1908.*

*Turbines in the
powerhouse of the
Mississippi River
Power Company
in Keokuk, ca.
1912–1913.
H. N. Anschutz,
photographer.*

Joe's cement gang
paving the side-
walks and working
on the sewers in
Malvern in 1906.
Allen Wortman
Collection.

A street sprinkler in Humboldt, ca. 1910.

A paving crew at work on the west side of the square in Greenfield in August 1911. 6 × 9½.

July 24, 1907

There are more automobiles going through here this summer than ever before. Hardly a fine day passes, but what a person can see one or more strange autos loaded with people, whizzing through town at a rapid pace.

—Diary of Joshua Williams of Lime Springs

In these days of closed cars and windshields, what comparison for protection was a mere low dashboard. We'd arrive at our destination with speckled faces and splotches of mud on our hair and clothes. Great effort was made to get through with the milk to the creamery, and the wagon wheels would be solid with thick mud to the hubs.

—"Mud," a reminiscence by Edith Mather of Cedar County, ca. 1939, p. 1

Women out for a drive, possibly near Davenport, ca. 1910. Howard Neff album.

The time since then has not been long, ten years ago an automobile was a rarity and a curiosity; neighbor women telephoned to those further down the road to look out and see the strange contraption. Anguished drivers, who saw death staring them in the face, clutched, with desperate grip the reins which restrained their frantic horses; chickens, with motions gauged to the slower speed of horse drawn vehicles, made futile rushes and died under the wheels of Juggernaut; barking dogs miscalculated the time necessary for retreat and barked no more forever. So the occasional motorist was hated by the farmers with an intense hatred.

—"Country Roads and Motor Cars," by Hortense Butler Heywood of Peterson, ca. 1910–1915

Men pulling an auto out of the mud at Wellman. 3½ × 5 postcard.

An automobile drive down a country road, ca. 1915.

The Nemaha Auto Company. Murle Abernathy, the manager, is at the left. 3½ × 5 postcard.

The interior of an auto garage in Eagle Grove, ca. 1920. "No children allowed in here unless accompanied by parents." Klassie Collection.

Bell Telephone line troubleshooters near Maquoketa in 1905. Original owned by Genevieve Hartman.

Ethel Howe, a telephone operator in Nemaha, 1918.

The old party telephone line system . . . was really an efficient local method of communication. Each rural community usually owned their own party line, and they kept care of it, and the line would run into a local town where they could make connections with other local party lines and with the rest of the world.

. . . We had emergency rings. If you had a fire or emergency in the home, someone was sick, you'd ring this emergency ring. It'd ring into everyone that was on that line. If anyone in the local town had a promotional sale, he'd ring this promotional ring and it'd be advertised free of nothing.

—Oral history interview with Harold Donham of Iowa City, conducted by Alvin Schroeder on March 21, 1977

[Ollie Ladd] was first rural mail carrier. Mail route out of Killduff was established in 1903. . . . Ollie gave up route in about a year and Irving Irish took over. . . . Mr. Irish had to heat a soap stone to put at his feet in the buggy and wear a heavy fur coat and a fur cap. He had two horses—used one horse on the forenoon route and the other horse on the afternoon route.
—Reminiscence by Mae Coggins of Killduff, January 1964

A rural free delivery buggy in Wellman, ca. 1900.

*Women listening to
the radio, ca. 1920.
5 × 7, Alice Mary
Gifford Collection.*

*The first Orpheum
Theater in Sioux
City, ca. 1915. Al-
bertype Company
Collection.*

Our central thought in establishing this institution [Sunnyside Farm] is to emphasize the social life on the farm. One of the reasons why Iowa lost in rural population the last few years was the lack of social life on the farm. . . .

The institution is to be essentially a big farmers' club, to which all within traveling distance will belong. The people can use the public hall for what meetings they like. The farmers can meet there to hear a lecture on soil fertility, their wives can use the hall for a quilting bee, the young people can gather there for party or dance. . . .

The library will be equipped to suit the varying tastes of all ages and dispositions and in it visitors can enjoy hours of quiet reading or study. In the laboratory will be equipment with which the young farmer can make simple tests of his soil, his feeds,

his seeds, and thereby make his farming more definite. The swimming pool, the tennis courts, the baseball diamond will be open to those inclined to sports. . . .

Enough moving pictures, good entertainments and other forms of light amusement will be offered at "The Camp" that the showy side of town life will not rob this country institution of any of its popularity. And there will be, too, lectures by experts out from the state college on problems of farming and household work, discussions of topics of liberal culture and any number of attractions.

It is to be simply their center of amusement, sociability and culture.

—Conger Reynolds in the Des Moines *Sunday Register and Leader*, September 27, 1914

Esther L. Mendenhall with her baby, Iowa City, ca. 1854. The original is a one-sixth plate daguerreotype.

EPILOGUE

Photographs are cultural artifacts capable of adding a new dimension and balance to the interpretation of history. By examining the photographers' choice of subjects and by studying their artistic styles, we can surmise what mattered most to them and to the society in which they lived. By briefly tracing the history of photography, we can learn who Iowa's photographers were, gain insights into how they created images, and explore the reasons why our ancestors created a visual record of their lives.

The development of photography in Iowa as both an artistic medium and a documentary record closely paralleled the spread of this new craft around the world. The invention of the daguerreotype occurred at the very time Iowa was first settled. From 1839 through the 1860s, daguerreotypes were the principal mode of photography, and although used primarily for portraiture, rare landscape views do exist (Isaac Wetherby's, for example). The image was created by covering a thin plate of copper with a highly polished, mirrorlike coating of silver. The surface was sensitized with iodine vapors and then exposed in a camera for several minutes. Long exposure times meant that any movement, in the scene or on the part of the subject, would blur the picture. The delicate surface of the plate was then covered by a piece of glass, framed by a decorative copper matte, and encased in a small hinged case made of leather or gutta-percha.

By the time daguerreotypists like John Plumbe (in Dubuque in 1840) or Isaac Wetherby (in Iowa City by 1854) reached the Iowa frontier, daguerreotypy was a well-refined craft. Continual experimentation with camera and lens construction, improved methods of lighting, and new chemical processes made it possible for any industrious person to learn and practice the art. Galleries were established wherever large segments of the population settled. It is difficult to trace the complete history of these pioneers in Iowa, but they left a record of the determined faces of the people who settled this region.

Daguerreotypist's wagon, ca. 1845–1850. Original one-sixth plate daguerreotype owned by George Goeldner.

It was a natural step for Iowa photographers to adopt ambrotype and tintype portraiture when these methods were introduced in the 1850s. Rarely used for landscape views, ambrotypes were actually collodion negatives on glass. The image became positive when a black backing of paper, velvet, or paint was placed behind the image. Because of the fragile glass, ambrotypes were also housed in protective cases. Unlike daguerreotypes, which have a reflective surface, ambrotypes have a creamy white look. Tintypes, appearing in the late 1850s, were collodion positives made directly on a thin sheet of lacquered iron. A very inexpensive form of photography, tintypes were especially popular in rural areas. All three of these early methods produced one-of-a-kind photos with a reversed image. On some of these early images, gold leaf was applied to buttons or jewelry worn by the subject, while others were hand tinted.

By the 1850s the use of a transparent collodion negative to produce multiple prints had revolutionized photography. Most of the prints made during the period from 1855 to 1895 were printed on albumen paper. The carte de visite portrait and stereograph landscape views became widely available and expanded people's knowledge of the world. Fancy velvet-covered and embossed leather albums with metal clasps became the rage, and family portraits were frequently arranged alongside portraits of prominent national figures like Abraham Lincoln.

Still, picture taking was limited to a few skilled artisans, to adventurous frontier photographers, and to those who practiced in the local portrait studio. Equipment was cumbersome, and taking a photograph required a good deal of preparation. A photographer used a large-format camera, set up a tripod to hold the camera steady, and had

A pioneer Iowa photographer, possibly Timothy W. Townsend, photographed by Isaac A. Wetherby, both of Iowa City, ca. 1859–1860. Putnam Museum.

to carry heavy (yet fragile) glass plate negatives. Before each snap of the shutter, the photographer coated a glass plate with a thin layer of collodion emulsion. This "wet plate" served as the negative for the upcoming photo. Glass negatives carried a high risk of failure and had to be chemically processed immediately after the picture was taken, necessitating the use of a portable darkroom, usually in a tent or wagon, if the photographer was working in the field. In the Society's collections, the studio work of Wetherby and D. C. Hale offers the only remaining evidence from this early period of photography in the state. Wetherby's plates are especially intriguing, as one can see how unevenly he applied the collodion to the surface of the plate, giving a graphic example of how difficult it was to coat the entire surface, including the edges, smoothly.

B.M.H.S. and her 5x8 Tripod Camera

The invention of the "dry plate" process around 1880 eliminated much of the inconvenience in taking pictures. Photographers could buy prepackaged glass plate negatives on which the gelatin emulsion layer had been applied mechanically. Even though dry plates required one-eighth of the time of wet plates, long exposures were still necessary. Serious amateurs could take outdoor photographs easily, and with some patience interior shots were possible (note Bertha Shambaugh's, for example). Albumen paper was sensitized by floating it in a solution, and it would darken once it was exposed to daylight. No chemical development was needed with printing-out paper unless the photographer wanted to tone the image.

Most nineteenth-century prints were contact prints, not enlargements, since so much outdoor light was required to expose the print. Printing frames held the negative and sensitized paper in close contact during exposure, which lasted from a few minutes to several hours. In the years from 1885 to 1910, amateur photographers sometimes made cyanotypes, or blueprint images, to test the negative's quality before making a final print on higher-quality paper. Less expensive machine-coated albumen paper became available in the 1880s, which improved the quality and consistency of the photographers' work. Snapshots were shared with neighbors and friends or pasted into the family photo album. With the proliferation of homemade photos, a new style of photo album emerged, offering a more informal commentary on the lives of the subjects.

As late as 1920, many photographers continued to use glass plate negatives. Professional photographers (like D. C. Hale) often clung to the methods of the past, using glass plate negatives for their studio work. The size of the plates commonly used (4 × 5, 5 × 7, and 7 × 9 inches) meant that photographers still used large-format cameras, usually with tripods. Photographers employing this arduous method were diligent in setting up complicated equipment, especially when they tracked down subjects outdoors. Still, their technical skill and artistic talents resulted in a body of incomparable negatives, rich in historical detail.

The fad of photography had already taken a firm hold on Iowans by the 1890s, when hand-held cameras came into vogue, simplifying photography and making it widely accessible. With the introduction of flexible roll film and smaller cameras, more "shutterbugs" appeared, opening new vistas for self-expression. Rapid shutter speeds allowed the photographer to capture candid, unplanned shots of people in a variety of settings. People built makeshift darkrooms in their homes for processing film. In the late 1890s, "gaslight paper"—paper that could be both exposed and processed by the light of gaslights—came into widespread use. Photographers like E. M. Clark created inexpensive postcard-sized prints that could be mailed to others or even sold locally. After 1905, most photographers switched to printing on developing-out paper. The negative and paper were exposed to a weak light in a darkroom, and the image appeared during the chemical development of the paper. Though by the turn of the century film could be conveniently processed at the local drugstore, more ambitious hobbyists continued to develop their negatives and prints at home.

The first flexible roll film, in use from 1889 to 1903, was nitrate-based and somewhat flimsy, and it had a tendency to curl tightly. Nitrate film in use from 1903 to 1939 was less likely to curl, but the negatives are susceptible to deterioration as the chemicals decompose. By 1939, "safety" film had arrived on the scene. The introduction of 35-mm film in the 1920s led to an expanded use of the photographic medium by an even broader spectrum of the population. Bromide developing-out paper, with a faster speed, became popular when people wanted to make enlargements of small camera negatives.

Throughout the period from 1860 to 1920, there is ample evidence that photographers took their technique seriously and wanted to improve their skills. Since aperture size and exposure time were not automatically set but had to be calculated for each

MARTIN MORRISON'S FIRST HOME IN ARNES IA.
In the Wintertime. Ames

Martin Morrison's first home in Ames, 1886. Note the photographic equipment. From a stereograph.

Self-portrait of Herbert H. Smith with his camera, reflected in a mirror, Iowa City, ca. 1896. Sanders family photo album.

E. M. Clark with her camera, Ruthven, ca. 1915. E. M. Clark Collection, original owned by Glenna Brott.

shot, serious photographers carefully noted exposure times and lighting conditions. Negative envelopes were usually stamped with blank lines for technical notes. Amateurs studied the many photography manuals published by supply companies and kept up on the latest developments in the medium.

Although a few Iowa photographers (like Frank E. Foster) later experimented with moving pictures, films taken before 1920 are rare indeed and have not been preserved in libraries or archives around the state. Still, the iconographic record of Iowa's past has a diverse base that includes not only photographs but also posters, broadsides, and advertisements as well as the lithographs, engravings, photogravures, and halftone illustrations used for newspapers, magazines, and other periodicals. County histories, town centennial histories created in the 1960s and 1970s, high school and college yearbooks, and other printed sources provide a wealth of historical images, expanding our perceptions of Iowa's past. Researchers are continually amazed by the breadth of experience photographed by Iowans and the level of sophistication they achieved with their photography.

Photographs can be considered a form of autobiography because through them people reconstruct or replicate a vision of their own existence. In comparing collections of multiple images from various families or from one photographer's career, a pattern emerges. We find similarities in the subject matter portrayed. We discover the photographer's agenda and biases. Her or his particular sensitivities and role within the community or within the family determine what is selected for photographing. Of course, the limits of technology and social convention govern every photographer's intent as well.

Family photographers, both in town and in the countryside, are well represented in the Society's photo archives. We are best able to explore the social context in which photographers worked and the material contents of a middle-class family home by examining these larger, more comprehensive collections. The vision of daily life created by these photographers helps form a general viewpoint or consensus of cultural imagery. The pattern that emerges verifies that certain stylistic trends prevailed and that people seemingly were inspired to take pictures for similar reasons. After viewing countless images showing pride in material wealth—for example, the ownership of a new automobile, a house, or one of the other rewards of hard work—we sense the importance most people placed on obtaining a higher standard of living. With a photograph we can witness the symbolic and sentimental self-expressions that offer clues about cultural values.

We also need to keep in mind what we are *not* seeing. Obviously, not all areas of life

The Rossiter Photo Gallery with skylight, Riceville, ca. 1890. Charles Rossiter operated this gallery from about 1888 to 1924. Original owned by Martha Dalton.

The Vosburg Studio in Osage in the 1890s. Julian A. Douglas engaged in the photography business here until his death in 1910.

are covered. Illegal behavior (gambling, prostitution, fighting, violent crime), health care and personal hygiene (pregnancy or childbirth, disease, or disability), and private social customs and taboos are not commonly photographed. There are few views of activities inside dwellings, since these were difficult to capture with the available film, cameras, and lighting. We may see people with reading materials or handiwork, but many more photos show stark, peopleless interiors. In other words, there was much more to life than the photographs portray. With only black-and-white images, we have no idea of how colorful life was unless we study other sources. Things we might take for granted or expect to find based on photos taken in our own time are not likely to

C. J. Daugherty's Capital City Photo Studio wagon and two traveling photographers, Rolly (left) and Johnny Foster from Earlham, ca. 1880. Olda and Ivey Barrett are on top of the wagon. State Historical Society of Iowa, Des Moines.

be present in this era of photography. People often concoct some notion or vision of what they should find in a photo archive, only to be disappointed that those views were seldom created.

Who were Iowa's photographers from 1860 to 1920? With few exceptions (Duren Ward and Paul Bartsch, for example), these photographs were not taken by social reformers or by a government agency documenting social conditions. The majority were taken by commercial photographers who made a living from studio photography, creating portraits of local residents. Others traveled around the area, offering to photograph farmers and their homesteads or helping to promote the town's businesses by photographing company employees or the interiors of stores or factory buildings. Photos of scenic wonders, public buildings, and landmarks were reproduced for sale, sometimes in the local railway station. The commercial photographer, along with skilled amateurs in less-populated areas, helped to establish the permanent documentary record of the community and its inhabitants, photographing memorable occasions while also recording the evolution of Main Street.

A total of 185 photographers appeared in a statewide list of proprietors of photo studios published in 1865. By 1880, *Polk's Iowa State Gazetteer* was listing 223, and in 1900 more than 580 photographers' names appeared. While this list is not complete, we know that professional photographers could be found in nearly every town in Iowa and that many towns had more than one photographer. Unlike many other activities in this

J. M. Stonestreet, a professional photographer, with his camera, Grinnell, 1895.

period, photography as a profession was open to both men and women, and a quarter to a third of the proprietors of professional studios were women.

A more complete profile of the photographers who operated studios in Iowa will emerge soon. Researchers will be able to track and analyze information on Iowa photographers and their photographic legacy. Alan Schroder began the project by compiling hundreds of data sheets for a directory of Iowa photographers before 1900. His work coincided with the efforts of JoAnn Burgess, who was also developing a statewide index to photographers, and John Zeller, who concentrated his research on Des Moines and Polk County photographers. Scouring city directories, state gazetteers, atlases, county histories, census records, tax lists, probate records, and even the imprint on the

T. W. Townsend's photo gallery on Clinton Street in Iowa City in the 1870s. Note the display rack on the sidewalk at the lower right, showing photographs. From a stereograph.

photographers' mounts, these persistent researchers gathered detailed information on most of Iowa's nineteenth-century practitioners. Work by Keith Eiten and others contributed to the expanding file. JoAnn Burgess has now designed an impressive computer data base to automate access to this information, unleashing a valuable resource with tremendous potential for historians investigating Iowa's photographic heritage.

The appendix that follows highlights some of the more important collections from the State Historical Society of Iowa in Iowa City that represent the work of Iowa's photographers, both professional and amateur. An enormous number of precious historical photographs exists in the state, yet there are few systematic efforts to identify and preserve these documents for researchers. In this book I have sought to present a small but representative sample of them to inspire people to collect and share our visual link to the past.

NOTES ON THE PHOTOGRAPH COLLECTIONS

The *Albertype Company Collection* consists of 447 nitrate negatives dating from 1915 to 1920. They were produced by a Brooklyn, New York, company that sold souvenir postcards and booklets. The views of twenty-two Iowa towns include businesses, street scenes, parks, residential areas, schools, churches, and libraries. Among the towns represented are Ames, Sioux City, Keokuk, Storm Lake, Mason City, Mount Pleasant, Oskaloosa, Clear Lake, Nevada, and Sabula.

Though not a photographer herself, *Jessie White Anderson* was a North Liberty woman who collected historical photographs of her community. Local businesses, neighboring farmsteads, and community life are portrayed in the collection, donated by her daughter, Delma Dale Dever.

Frederick J. Bandholtz (1877–?) was a Des Moines photographer who traveled around Iowa and the West to create panoramic views of Main Streets to sell as folding souvenir postcards. He documented fifty-one Iowa cities in exquisite fashion, and the original 1907 photographs, now quite fragile, can be found in the Library of Congress. Little is known about this Illinois native, but the 1900 census indicates that his wife, Mary, and he had a three-month-old daughter named Margaret. In 1900 he was employed by the Des Moines Rug and Carpet Cleaning Works, but from 1903 to 1913 city directories list his occupation as photographer. Surviving images indicate that he took his circuit camera as far as Lexington, Nebraska, and to towns in eastern Idaho in 1909. Views of selected Iowa towns are available as reproductions in the collections of the State Historical Society.

Paul Bartsch documented the pearl button industry along the Mississippi River. The seventy-eight glass plate negatives, taken sometime between 1900 and 1912, but especially in 1907, include interior views of factories showing women sorting buttons and working with heavy machinery. Bartsch was hired by the U.S. Bureau of Fisheries to investigate the depletion of mussels in the river and its potential impact on local industry.

William Bentler created images of farm life in the area surrounding Houghton and Pilot Grove in about 1910. The 104 glass plate negatives offer views of farming activities and neighborhood socializing from the intimate perspective of a farmer and amateur photographer. John Bentler donated the collection.

Edith Mary (E. M.) Clark (1884–1963) was born in Ruthven; by her early twenties she had already earned a reputation as the "town photographer" even though she had no studio and her darkroom was a hallway in the family home. Clark made postcard-sized prints, embossing the white border along one side with "E. M. Clark, Ruthven, Iowa," and placing them in local shop windows. A collection of postcards and three small photo albums reveal Clark as an artist of unusual talent, possessing a keen eye and a sensitive imagination. Traveling around in a buggy, she created a delightful portrait of everyday life. Her playful, staged images of children are especially charming. After she eloped in 1912 to marry Dale Brott, she devoted little time to photography. The mother of six children, she also helped raise some orphans and a relative's children. Parts of the collection were donated by the Glenna Brott family.

Will Cundill (1855–1942) left a sizable legacy from his years as a professional photographer in Maquoketa. Over 600 glass plate negatives and nearly 100 photographic postcards dating from 1917 to 1935 are preserved at the State Historical Society of Iowa. His portrait studio work is largely unidentified, but town scenes document stores, community groups, parades, and firemen's tournaments. Cundill was known as a poet, and as an 1889 sketch of Cundill's life in a Jackson County history indicates, he was fully engaged in the life of the community. His son Frank, who homesteaded near Timber Lake, South Dakota, used his skills as a photographer to document pioneer conditions in the Dakotas, sending his glass plates back to Iowa for processing and printing. The Cundill Collection was donated by Harry Hicks.

The *Farley and Loetscher Company* was a millworking firm operating out of Dubuque and other Iowa towns at the turn of the century. More than a hundred photos, used primarily for advertising, accompany the firm's business records, providing superb images of workers in the factory and views of millwork products on display in homes and offices. One series shows views taken at various stages in the construction of the company headquarters. The firm's trade catalogs, which it published jointly with other prominent sash and door companies in Iowa, are a treasure trove for people seeking examples of designs for windows, woodwork, storefronts, and other architectural details and ornamentation.

Mary Jane Chapman Fawcett (1856–1938) of Sandyville began to document everyday life in her rural neighborhood in about 1910, traveling around in a buggy. She took lessons in photography from Mrs. Lidd Zarley of Zarley's Art Studio in Indianola and used her kitchen as a darkroom. Her best images show

farming activities, although she was called upon to take pictures at family gatherings and town celebrations as well. She was the mother of eleven children and led a busy life as a farm woman. The original nitrate negatives are owned by her daughter, Eden Fawcett Trotter.

Frank E. Foster (1866–1943) of Iowa Falls left a collection of 648 glass plate negatives that beautifully document small-town life in Iowa from 1895 to 1910. Foster was a newspaperman, insurance agent, and town booster whose hobby was photography. His portrait of life in Iowa Falls is unsurpassed for the comprehensive range of topics it covers. There are outstanding views of local artisans, circuses and carnivals, parades, celebrations, houses, mills, rivers, and the railroad. The more intimate, private side of domestic life and children's activities becomes visible. The information and identification provided with the images, largely due to the efforts of the Foster family, enhance the value of the collection. John Foster donated the collection.

The *Gabelmann Collection* is comprised of photographs taken in the 1910s, primarily by Bertha Gabelmann or her relative, Karl Walther. Gabelmann's handwritten diaries cover a period of fifty years, and the snapshot photographs add an important visual dimension to the study of her life. She faced challenges as an unmarried woman running the family farm with her sister. Images of work in the fields and routine chores around a farmstead show women planting in a cold frame, tapping the wine barrel, and butchering ducks. The origi-

nal nitrate negatives are owned by Constance Walther.

DeWitt Clinton (D. C.) Hale (1857–1934) practiced his art in Elkader after learning his trade under a Dubuque photographer named Nichols. The collection of 372 glass plate negatives dates from 1879 to 1930. Sixty rare wet plate negatives with very fragile layers of emulsion are stereograph views from around 1880. Hale photographed mills, schools, churches, houses, businesses, the courthouse, and the Turkey River, along with dozens of community groups, including GAR veterans and athletic teams. Through the generosity of his daughter, Grace Hale, and the efforts of Bill Witt, the photographic treasury of D. C. Hale has been preserved. Witt's article in the *Iowan* magazine in March 1978 summarizes Hale's work.

The *Huftalen Papers* encompass an extensive manuscript collection most noted for the diaries of Emily Hawley Gillespie (1838–1888). Diaries, scrapbooks, and other writings provide a record of the life and career of her daughter, Sarah Huftalen (1865–1952?), a teacher and school superintendent. Several photograph albums illustrate rural education in Iowa in the first two decades of the twentieth century, including farm camps and teachers' institutes. One album shows activities in a one-room school, the Arbor Vitae Summit School at Oneida in Delaware County, including a series on the beautification of the school grounds (which is featured in the Spring 1987 *Palimpsest*).

The *Paul Juhl Collection* is especially significant because it contains the earliest and highest-quality landscape photographs ever taken in Iowa. The stereographs offer a clear picture of life in Iowa's communities during the formative years from the late 1860s to the 1880s. Business districts, recreational activities, public institutions, houses, bridges, memorable occasions, and disastrous events were photographed by as many as 150 professionals from all areas of the state. More than 960 stereographs of Iowa have been identified, and a growing collection of 400 reproductions and copy negatives is available to researchers.

The *William Kock Collection* is comprised of 335 images created from 1910 to 1920 by a farmer and amateur photographer from Boone County. The photographer's original log, neatly kept in small handwriting, and the labeled envelopes allow the photos to be completely identified and accurately dated. Included are excellent views of such fieldwork as draining and tiling, blasting stumps, planting, and harvesting. As in other collections created by farmers, there are numerous images of typically male activities such as trapshooting, hunting, and fishing. Informal portraits of family and friends engaged in horseplay are also common. The glass plate and nitrate negatives are owned by Craig Davenport.

The *Larrabee Collection* is an enormous resource of more than 1,500 original photographs taken from the 1860s through at least the 1920s. Governor William Larrabee was one of the wealthiest and most influential men in nineteenth-century Iowa. A pioneer miller in the state,

he amassed a fortune from land speculation, became an expert on railroad issues, and forged a prominent role in Republican politics. His wife, Anna, and their seven children led the privileged life of a gentry class, sophisticated beyond the means of most Iowans. Photos, usually taken by the children, portray family activities around Montauk, their home in Clermont, and include views of the interior, exterior, and grounds. Along with more than a hundred formal studio portraits and informal snapshots, there are eleven photo albums, some with wonderful travel photos from a 1901 grand tour of Europe, Egypt, and the Holy Land.

The *Mather-Bush Papers* and the *John Elbert (J. E.) Mather Collection* offer a remarkable glimpse into the lives of several generations of a Quaker family from Cedar County. Much of the family's history from 1860 to 1920 has been compiled into eight volumes titled "A Pictorial History of the Samuel Mather Family at Evergreens." These scrapbook albums include photographs, other illustrations, documents, newsclippings, and even scraps of fabric from clothing or upholstery. One member of the clan, J. E. Mather, studied photography under Jacoby and Barnes, pioneer photographers in West Liberty, and then ran a studio in Anamosa for a time. Scenes of the family camping along the Cedar River, swimming, or entertaining themselves at home are rich in detail. The original glass plate negatives are in the hands of J. E. Mather's son, Merlin Mather, but ninety-five of the most interesting photos were loaned for copying.

The *Fred Maurer Collection* of 116 prints made from glass plate negatives dates from about 1899 to 1914, though most are from 1900 to 1902. There are views of his hometown of Wilton, bicycling, horse racing, and his family's home environment. He evidently used a flash for some of the interior shots. A companion collection consists of twenty-nine prints taken by his nephew, Art Wacker. The views of the interior of the Maurer home, the Wacker family, and bird's-eye views of Wilton all date from 1904. The original glass plate negatives are privately owned.

George Muegge collected photos relating to Communia, which began as a communal society in Clayton County in the 1840s. Though its existence was short-lived, surviving documents tell about the aims of Joseph Venus and his followers. The handful of images from around 1890 capture people at work in the wheat fields and at play in the local Turner society, an organization of gymnasts and athletes.

Duluth Pieper (1897–1950?) was a Clayton County photographer who is represented by a collection of about 200 glass plate negatives dating from about 1905 to 1926. Not much is known about Pieper, although the 1915 state census indicates that he lived at home near McGregor and was then eighteen years old, "illegitimate," and "crippled." He may have taken up his hobby at a young age, creating a typical array of farm photographs of such subjects as fieldwork, barn construction, houses, the circus, and precious views of farm animals. The original envelopes for the negatives provide detailed information about his lens, brand of plate, paper, and developer as well as the time of day, lighting conditions, and exposure time. This collection was acquired with the assistance of Bill Witt.

Gerdjanssen Rickels (1874–1948), a Lutheran minister and the son of German immigrants, grew up near Scotch Grove. His passion for photography began in 1897, and the 143 images in the Society's collections are but a sample of his best work from 1917 to 1930. The engaging portrait of family life in a rural parish offers intimate views of household activities, kitchen work, laundering, child rearing, and playtime for his two children, Lenore and Robbie. An article in the Winter/Spring 1987 *Annals of Iowa* offers a summary of Rickels's life and work written by the donor, his daughter, Lenore M. Salvaneschi.

Nels L. Roslien (1879–1958), the son of Norwegian immigrants, was a bachelor farmer who portrayed rural life around Kensett from about 1905 to 1915. The 438 dry plate negatives offer extensive documentation of daily life on the farmsteads surrounding the Roslien farm. Although Nels was strictly an amateur photographer, neighbors often requested that he take pictures of a favorite team of horses, a new house, a new automobile, or an event at the local school. Images of farm equipment and machinery, barns, animal care, and domestic chores are among the most outstanding. Almost half of the photos are portraits of family and friends, often taken with a sheet or bedspread as a backdrop. Some plates

contain up to four different images of the same person. Most unusual for a collection like this are a series of copy negatives of mildly pornographic images and one photo of a nude woman. The donor of the collection, Al Sparby, owns his uncle's large-format rosewood camera and tripod.

Leonard A. Schwinn (1862–1936) came to Red Oak in the late 1880s and worked as a shoe salesman and an employee of the Thomas Murphy Calendar Company. His wife, Kate, and he had two sons, Byron, born in 1895, and Walter, born in 1901. The 119 glass plate negatives that survive are a testament to his skills as a photographer dedicated to recording not only his family's recreational activities but also life in his community. Exquisitely detailed photographs show picnics, watermelon parties, and nut gathering in a local grove. Local historians treasure the views of schools, the county courthouse, mills, bridges, stores, fire ruins, the telephone switchboard, floods on the Nishnabotna River, house exteriors and interiors, and fairs. The building of the Chicago, Burlington and Quincy Railroad and the activities of soldiers from Company M—leaving the train station during the Spanish-American War and returning to march through a victory arch—were of great interest to Schwinn. The collection was donated by his son, Walter K. Schwinn.

Effie Seward lived in Bentonsport and created 130 glass plate negatives dating from about 1903 to 1905. Though little information exists about her life, this amateur photographer's collection offers rare views

of this southeastern Iowa community. Photographs show floods on the Des Moines River, repair work on the railroad, landscape shots, and children at play. More skilled at snapshot portraits, Seward conveys an intimate relationship with her subjects. The glass plate negatives were brought to the Society by Oneita Fisher.

Bertha Maude Horack Shambaugh (1871–1953) was an accomplished photographer who received her first camera as a high school graduation present in 1889. Though she herself took pictures, primarily from 1889 to 1910, the collection includes more than 1,100 photographs and nearly 500 negatives, many taken by professional photographers. As a young woman, Shambaugh carried her heavy camera equipment around Iowa City and to the Amana Society, where she created the first visual record of its communal life. Noted as a historian of the Amana colonies, Shambaugh was also a high school teacher of natural science and a fledgling artist. She shared an interest in state and local history with her husband, Benjamin F. Shambaugh, who was superintendent of the State Historical Society and head of the University of Iowa's political science department. Together they served as hosts to the many distinguished visitors who came to Iowa City. The extensive collection of images demonstrates her awareness of the importance of photography for preserving a more complete historical record. An article in the March/April 1980 *Palimpsest* provides more background information on Shambaugh, whose papers and photographs are in the

University of Iowa Archives as well as at the State Historical Society.

Jessie Field Shambaugh (1881–1971) was an educator dedicated to improving the quality of life for rural youth. Her clubs and farm camps were forerunners of the 4-H movement. Photos taken from 1909 to 1912 depict classes in home economics, vocational training, horticulture and livestock judging, and the young men who formed road-dragging crews. These images and family portraits were loaned for copying by Ruth Watkins. A separate collection concentrates on her father, the famous nurseryman Henry Field, and his family.

The *Thompson Family Papers* (1843–1968) contain commercial photographs that reflect the lives of the prosperous merchants, bankers, and land barons of Forest City. The entrepreneur Jasper Thompson and his son, Burt, built a small empire in Winnebago County, even naming a town after themselves. The pictorial record of their achievements is preserved in professional photographs of Burt's years as a Grinnell College student, newly established banks, their residences, travel photos, the Flax Palace in Forest City, and their philanthropic efforts, like Sunnyside Farm. The collection was donated by Bruce S. Thompson.

The *Ward-Mesquakie Collection* contains 119 photographs of the Mesquakie Indians and their settlement in Tama County. Duren H. Ward spent two months at the settlement in 1905, studying and documenting tribal life. He hired J. S. Moore, a Toledo photographer, to take portraits of the tribal members

on August 14, 1905, and many of the Mesquakie dressed in traditional clothing. Although the vast majority of the images are portraits, there are also informal views of the settlement and housing conditions there. Ward and his assistant may have taken some of the photos, and some were borrowed from George Moran and John W. Lamb.

William Adams (W. A.) Warren (1868–1947) came to West Liberty in 1894. He is represented by a collection of 166 glass plate negatives dated between 1895 and 1917. Since Warren traveled in the area, there are also views related to Iowa City and Nichols. The revealing photographs show houses, railroads, churches, and family outings and reunions. Warren and a brother were carpenters and contractors who built a number of homes. He also documented his woodworking hobby and played tricks with the camera by double exposing the plate. More than a thousand dry plate negatives are still in private hands.

Isaac A. Wetherby (1819–1904) was a pioneer artist in Iowa, working first as a painter and then with daguerreotypes, ambrotypes, and the wet plate process. A dozen rare views of Iowa City street scenes from the mid 1850s were among the earliest photographs taken in the state. He operated a studio from 1859 to 1874, although his artistic pursuits eventually led him away from his wife and family in Iowa City. The 190 wet plate negatives show large groups posing in his studio under skylights or on the steps of Old Capitol. The majority (about 160) are portraits, and some

are positive collodions or ambrotypes that were never put in cases. A daybook, letters, and other papers document his career. The Library of Congress has additional images, the New-York Historical Society has Wetherby oil paintings, and the Putnam Museum in Davenport holds more wet plate negatives and documents.

Women's Clubs Community Heritage Scrapbooks were the result of a project sponsored by the State Historical Society and the Iowa Federation of Women's Clubs in the late 1950s. The results are impressive—64 albums containing 2,900 historical photographs that date from 1860 to 1959. Some of the best albums came from Clear Lake, Ames, Lamoni, Elgin, Jefferson, Greenfield, Humboldt, Nemaha, Mount Pleasant, Paullina, Webster, Kalona, Wellman, and Solon.

Allen Wortman, a Mills County newspaper editor and local historian, collected views of Malvern and the surrounding communities. Though the bulk of his collection is comprised of negatives from the files of the Malvern *Leader* from the 1940s to the 1960s, Wortman also made an effort to collect and copy turn-of-the-century views of Mills County.

BIBLIOGRAPHY

IOWA HISTORY

Note: Historians have relied heavily on articles published in the *Iowa Journal of History and Politics*, the *Iowa Journal of History*, the *Palimpsest*, and the *Annals of Iowa*. These journals offer a wealth of information and a good starting point for the study of Iowa history.

Arden, Harvey. "Iowa, America's Middle Earth." *National Geographic*, May 1981, 603–29.

Atherton, Lewis. *Main Street on the Middle Border*. Bloomington: Indiana University Press, 1954.

Aurner, Clarence R. *History of Education in Iowa*. 5 vols. Iowa City: State Historical Society of Iowa, 1914–1920.

Behrman, Sara, comp. "Selected Sources on the Mesquakie Indians." *Research Papers* [Office of the State Archaeologist of Iowa] 8 (1983): 1–34.

Bergmann, Leola Nelson. *The Negro in Iowa*. Studies in Iowa History. Iowa City: State Historical Society of Iowa, 1969. Originally published in the *Iowa Journal of History and Politics*, January 1948.

Bogue, Allan G. *From Prairie to Corn Belt: Farming on the Illinois and Iowa Prairies in the Nineteenth Century*. Chicago: Quadrangle Books, 1963.

Burchfield, Robert, and Linda K. Kerber. "The Household: Conducted by Mrs. Nellie M. Rich." *Palimpsest* 61 (March/April 1980): 42–55.

Chase, Edwin Percy. "Forty Years of Main Street." *Iowa Journal of History and Politics* 34 (July 1936): 227–61.

Clark, Clifford Edward, Jr. *The American Family Home, 1800–1960*. Chapel Hill: University of North Carolina Press, 1986.

Cohen, Lizabeth A. "Embellishing a Life of Labor: An Interpretation of the Material Culture of American Working-Class Homes, 1885–1915." In *Material Culture Studies in America*, ed. Thomas J. Schlereth. Nashville: American Association for State and Local History, 1981.

Cooper, Tom C., ed. *Iowa's Natural Heritage*. Des Moines: Iowa Natural Heritage Foundation and the Iowa Academy of Science, 1982.

Cowan, Ruth Schwartz. "The 'Industrial Revolution' in the Home: Household Technology and Social Change in the Twentieth Century." In *Material Culture Studies in America*, ed. Thomas J. Schlereth. Nashville: American Association for State and Local History, 1981.

Dawson, Patricia, and David Hudson, comps. *Iowa History and Culture: A Bibliography of Materials Published between 1952 and 1986*. Ames: State Historical Society of Iowa in conjunction with the Iowa State University Press, 1989.

Gue, Benjamin F. *History of Iowa*. 4 vols. New York: Century History Company, 1903.

Harlan, Edgar R. *A Narrative History of the People of Iowa*. 5 vols. Chicago: American Historical Society, 1931.

Kaplan, Wendy. *"The Art that is Life": The Arts & Crafts Movement in America, 1875–1920*. Boston: Museum of Fine Arts, 1987.

Kirschner, Don. *City and Country*. Westport, Conn.: Greenwood Press, 1970.

Koerselman, Gary. "The Quest for Community in Rural Iowa: Neighborhood Life in Early Middleburg History." *Annals of Iowa*, 3d ser., 41 (Summer 1972): 1006–1020.

Lingeman, Richard. *Small Town America: A Narrative History, 1620–Present*. New York: G. P. Putnam's Sons, 1980.

———. "The American Small Town: Where It Came From, What It Was, What It Is." Proceedings of the Symposium on the Small Town in America, Grinnell, Iowa: Grinnell College, 1989. Copy at the State Historical Society of Iowa, Iowa City.

Marsh, Margaret. "From Separation to Togetherness: The Social Construction of Domestic Space in American Suburbs, 1840–1915." *Journal of American History* 76 (September 1989): 506–27.

Morain, Thomas J. *Prairie Grass Roots: An Iowa Small Town in the Early Twentieth Century*. Ames: Iowa State University Press, 1988.

Noun, Louise R. *Strong-Minded Women: The Emergence of the Woman-Suffrage Movement in Iowa*. Ames: Iowa State University Press, 1969.

Persons, Stow. *American Minds*. Huntington, N.Y.: Robert E. Krieger, 1975.

Petersen, William J. *Iowa History*

Reference Guide. Iowa City: State Historical Society of Iowa, 1952.

Porter, Kenneth W., ed. "A Little Girl on an Iowa Forty, 1873–1880: Catherine Wiggins Porter." *Iowa Journal of History* 51 (April 1953): 131–55.

Purcell, L. Edward. "The Mesquakie Indian Settlement in 1905." *Palimpsest* 55 (March/April 1974): 34–55.

Rickoon, J. Sanford. *Threshing in the Midwest, 1820–1940: A Study of Traditional Culture and Technological Change.* Bloomington: Indiana University Press, 1988.

Rifkind, Carole. *Main Street: The Face of Urban America.* New York: Harper and Row, 1977.

Riley, Glenda. *Frontierswomen: The Iowa Experience.* Ames: Iowa State University Press, 1981.

Rogers, Earl M., comp. *A List of References for the History of Agriculture in Iowa.* Davis, Calif.: Agricultural History Center, University of California, Davis, 1979.

Ross, Earle. *Iowa Agriculture.* Iowa City: State Historical Society of Iowa, 1951.

Sage, Leland L. *History of Iowa.* Ames: Iowa State University Press, 1974.

Schlereth, Thomas J., ed. *Material Culture: A Research Guide.* Lawrence: University Press of Kansas, 1985.

———. *Material Culture Studies in America.* Nashville: American Association for State and Local History, 1981.

Schwieder, Dorothy. "Iowa: The Middle Land." In *Heartland: Midwestern History and Culture.* Bloomington: Indiana University Press, 1988.

———. *Black Diamonds: Life and Work in Iowa's Coal Mining Communities, 1895–1925.* Ames: Iowa State University Press, 1983.

———. *Patterns and Perspectives in Iowa History.* Ames: Iowa State University Press, 1973.

Schwieder, Dorothy, Thomas Morain, and Lynn Nielsen. *Iowa: Past to Present; The People and the Prairie.*

Ames: Iowa State University Press, 1989.

Stromquist, Shelton. "A Sense of Place." *History News*, April 1983, 17–20.

HISTORICAL
PHOTOGRAPHY

Bennett, Mary. "A Brief Career Leaves Its Mark: The Photographic Legacy of E. M. Clark." *Iowan*, Winter 1983, 47–49.

———. "Images of Victorian Iowa." *Palimpsest* 61 (March/April 1980): 34–41.

Borchert, James. "Analysis of Historical Photographs: A Method and a Case Study." *Studies in Visual Communication* 7, no. 4 (Fall 1981): 30–63.

———. "Historical Photo-Analysis: A Research Method." *Historical Methods* 15, no. 2 (Spring 1982): 35–44.

———. "Photographs and Historical Research: Prospects and Problems." Unpublished paper from Conference on Photographs and History, Center for the Study of Recent History of the United States, University of Iowa, April 21–22, 1989. Copy at the State Historical Society of Iowa, Iowa City.

Christian, Rebecca. "William Larrabee: Iowa's Outspoken Crusader for Reform." *Iowan*, Winter 1983, 11–19, 52–53.

Darrah, William C. *Cartes de Visite in Nineteenth Century Photography.* Gettysburg, Pa.: W. C. Darrah, 1981.

———. *The World of Stereographs.* Gettysburg, Pa.: W. C. Darrah, 1977.

"Duren Ward Mesquakie Photograph Exhibit." *News for Members*, Iowa State Historical Department, Spring 1982, 3.

Foster, Frank E., Collection Inventory, SHSI.

Hale, D. C., Collection Inventory, SHSI.

Malan, Nancy E. "Interpreting Historical Photographs: Pitfalls and Possibilities." *Picturescope* 26, no. 1 (Spring 1980): 9–11, 22.

Motz, Marilyn F. "Visual Autobiography: Photograph Albums of Turn-of-the-Century Midwestern Women." *American Quarterly* 41 (March 1989): 63–92.

Newhall, Beaumont. *The Daguerreotype in America*, 3d ed. New York: Dover, 1976.

———. *The History of Photography.* Rev. ed. New York: Museum of Modern Art, 1982.

Purcell, L. Edward. "The Ward-Mesquakie Photograph Collection." *Palimpsest* 55 (March/April 1974): 56–64.

Roslien, Nels L., Collection Inventory, SHSI.

Scharf, Aaron. *Art and Photography.* Baltimore: Penguin Books, 1974.

Schlereth, Thomas J. *Artifacts and the American Past.* Nashville: American Association for State and Local History, 1980.

Schwinn, Leonard A., Collection Inventory, SHSI.

Seale, William. *The Tasteful Interlude: American Interiors through the Camera's Eye.* New York: Praeger Publishers, 1975.

Shambaugh Collection Inventory, SHSI.

Stott, William. *Documentary Expression and Thirties America.* New York: Oxford University Press, 1973.

Taft, Robert. *Photography and the American Scene: A Social History, 1839–1889.* New York: Dover, 1964.

Talbot, George. *At Home: Domestic Life in the Post-Centennial Era, 1876–1920.* Madison: State Historical Society of Wisconsin, 1976.

Thomas, Alan. *Time in a Frame: Photography and the Nineteenth-Century Mind.* New York: Schocken, 1979.

Toole, K. Ross. *Montana: An Uncommon Land.* Norman: University of Oklahoma Press, 1973.

Trachtenberg, Alan. "Introduction: Photographs as Symbolic History." In *The American Image: Photographs*

from the National Archives,
1860–1960. New York: Pantheon
Books, 1979.

Vanderbilt, Paul. *Evaluating Historical
Photographs: A Personal Perspective.*
AASLH Technical Leaflet, no. 120.
Nashville: American Association for
State and Local History, 1979.

Warren, W. A., Collection Inventory,
SHSI.

Weinstein, Robert A., and Larry
Booth. *Collection, Use and Care of
Historical Photographs.* Nashville:
American Association for State and
Local History, 1979.

Welling, William B. *Collectors' Guide
to Nineteenth-Century Photographs.*
New York: Macmillan, 1976.

Witt, Bill. "The Photographic Legacy
of D. C. Hale." *Iowan,* March 1978,
36–43.

INDEX

Coover (photographer), 230, 236–239
Corn, 33, 52, 55–56
Cornell College, 179
Corwith, 71
Council Bluffs, 235
County courthouses, 134–135
Creameries, 70
Cress, Laura, 213
Creston, 193
Croquet, 244
Crozier, W. D., 198
Cultivators, 32
Cundill, Frank, 316
Cundill, Will, 315–316

Dams, 263, 288
Dancing, 176, 242
Daugherty, C. J., 312
Davenport, 182, 190, 291
Dawson, 52
Decorah, 39, 145, 215, 272, 277
Delta, 260
Dentists, 100
Des Moines, 81, 85, 94, 169, 187, 189, 191, 270, 315
DeWitt, 189
Doctors, 101
Dolen, J. O., 144
Donham, Harold, 47, 50, 55, 158, 242, 296
Donnellson, 32
Douglas, Julian A., 311
Drainage ditches, 42
Drugstores, 86, 87
Dry goods stores, 78, 89
Dubuque, 108, 114, 130, 131, 257, 268, 274, 316
Dyalls' Studios, 40
Dysart, 109, 131

Eagle Grove, 294
Earlham, 312
East Des Moines, 104
East Dubuque, Illinois, 274
Eberhart, H. C., 12
Eddyville, 163, 273
Edinger (photographer), 191
Eldora, 218
Electricity, 27, 37, 203–204, 222
Elevators, grain, 71, 81
Elgin, 31, 53, 178
Elkader, 143, 160, 316
Elliott, 92, 282–283
Emmetsburg, 192

Ethnic groups. *See* Immigrants
Extension Service. *See* Iowa State Extension Service

Fairfield, 83, 88
Fairs, 168, 169
Family life, 200–205, 218–221, 223, 226, 228, 254
Farley and Loetscher Company, 76, 114, 316
Farm buildings, 26, 32, 39
Farmers, 40
Farm labor. *See* Hired hands
Farm life, 24–30, 36, 52, 65, 263–266
Fawcett, Mary Jane Chapman, 316
Fenton, 278
Ferries, 274
Fertilizer, 44
Festivals, 159
Field, Henry, 75, 319
Fire companies, 196
Fires, 197
Fisher, Mary, 34, 100, 215, 248
Flaherty, Denise, 213
Floods, 198
Forest City, 207, 319
Forgrave, Grace Bouler, 211, 223
Fort Dodge, 107, 120, 121, 131
Fort Madison, 194, 195
Foster, Frank E., 63, 107, 166, 167, 175, 217, 218, 231, 232, 310, 316
Foundries, 125
Fourth of July, 139, 172, 177
Fraternal organizations, 138
Funerals, 258

Gabelmann, Bertha, or Karl Walther, 50, 52, 57, 60, 65, 219, 310, 316
Gambling, 137, 311
Games, 183
Gardening, 26, 65, 202, 204
Gender and traditional roles, 1, 24, 74, 201–202
General stores, 74, 78, 79
Giaque, Alfred T., 33, 63, 88
Gladbrook, 199
Glove factories, 132
Golf, 244
Good Roads Movement, 265
Gossip, 133, 183, 184
Granger movement, 29
Green County, 54, 64
Greenfield, 290
Grinnell, 313

Griswold, 61
Groceries, 73, 83–85, 94
Gun clubs, 182
Gypsum, 120, 121

Haines Brothers, 287
Haldeman (photographer), 61
Hale, DeWitt Clinton (D. C.), 160, 305, 307, 316
Hamilton (photographer), 164
Hardware stores, 89
Harness shops, 106
Hartman, Leah, 166, 181, 188, 196
Haugen, Gilbert, 221
Havelock, 186
Hawkins, 125
Heywood, Hortense Butler, 33, 38, 159, 170, 184, 292
Hicks, Carolyn, 208
High schools, 143, 144
Hired girls (housework), 27–28, 130, 215
Hired hands, 27
Hogs, 58–60
Holidays, 139, 146, 172, 177, 257
Homes: exteriors, 37, 62, 64, 66, 204, 206–210, 220, 259, 260; interiors, 200, 202–203, 224–240
Hopkinton, 86
Horse-drawn transportation, 68, 70–72, 80, 202, 262, 275, 290
Horse racing, 181
Horses, 26, 61, 80
Hospitals, 193
Hotels, 97, 98
Houghton, 315
House construction, 206
Housekeeping, 26, 130, 202, 208, 211–213, 215–218, 222
Huftalen, Sarah, 316
Humboldt, 44, 288, 290
Hunting, 243
Hyde, C. L., 109

Ice cream socials, 158
Ice making, 105, 209
Ice skating, 174
Ida County, 35
Ideals, 24, 202, 261
Immigrants, 5, 76, 137, 261, 263, 269
Independence, 181
Indianola, 316
Indians, 1–5
Interurbans, electric, 264, 268, 276, 287